FISKE
COUNTDOWN
⒯COLLEGE
41 TO-DO LISTS

and a Plan for Every Year of High School

EDWARD B. FISKE
BRUCE G. HAMMOND

SOURCEBOOKS, INC.
NAPERVILLE, ILLINOIS

Published by Sourcebooks, Inc.
P.O. Box 4410, Naperville, Illinois 60567-4410
(630) 961-3900
Fax: (630) 961-2168
www.sourcebooks.com

Library of Congress Cataloging-in-Publication Data

Hammond, Bruce G.
  Fiske countdown to college : 41 to-do lists and a plan for every year of high school / by Bruce G. Hammond and Edward B. Fiske.
    p. cm.
  1. Universities and colleges—United States—Admission—Handbooks, manuals, etc. 2. College student orientation—United States—Handbooks, manuals, etc. 3. High school students—United States—Handbooks, manuals, etc. I. Fiske, Edward B. II. Title.
  LB2351.2.H34 2009
  378.1'610973—dc22
                          2009012844

Printed and bound in the United States of America.
VP 10 9 8 7 6 5 4 3 2

contents

introduction: fasten your seat belts

Welcome to a unique phase of life: the college search. Young people are no longer kids but are not quite ready to be full-fledged adults. It is an in-between time. Parents, including many who are accustomed to doing things for their teens, must take a step back. Students, who have always relied on their parents to clear the way, must now step forward and chart their own path.

It is easier said than done. Any parent can pay lip service to the idea that students should take control, but when the chips are down, the urge to step in and make things right can be overwhelming. On the other hand, students constantly talk about wanting to be on their own, but as the college search heats up, they often hesitate just long enough to lure Mom or Dad into coming to the rescue. For many students, picking a college will be the first adult decision they make—and the real beginning of their higher education.

The purpose of this book is to help students to take charge and parents to understand their vital supporting role. For every crucial phase of the college search, we offer comprehensive "to-do" lists to help ease fears and eliminate uncertainty. The lists are written directly to students and/or parents. Specially marked items highlight the best resources on the Internet for the college search. Perhaps most importantly, the book includes scores of quotations from real students, parents, and high school counselors, who offer the ultimate insider's perspective on the college search. Listen carefully to their advice.

The college search has its share of stress, but when things get intense, remember the big picture. It isn't about getting into Big Name U or carrying on a family tradition. The college search is about launching a young person on the path to success and happiness. As long as families stay grounded in this reality, success is guaranteed.

grade

College seems a world away to most ninth graders. It takes imagination to picture yourself on a college campus when eleventh and twelfth graders look like giants. Parents are the ones who see college on the horizon, and they inevitably are the first to focus on the college search.

✔ GETTING A GOOD START

It's never too early for a parent to start thinking about the college admissions process, as long as you don't make too big a fuss about it. Tread lightly and get informed now—before the pressure heats up.

Control Your Anxiety

If you're already thinking about college, remember that your son or daughter is still adjusting to high school. Be gentle. Push too hard and you'll risk creating an oppositional dynamic that may last throughout the next four years and beyond.

Help Your Son or Daughter Make Choices

Some kids need a nudge to get involved in activities; others need help in narrowing down their commitments so they can focus on a few. It is better to establish leadership and distinction in a couple of activities than to dabble in many.

Do a Four-Year Plan

Some schools host an event for eighth graders and their parents to map out plans for high school. If yours does not, ask for a meeting with the guidance counselor, to include your son or daughter, to go over expectations for the next four years.

Assess Family Finances

Now is a great time to begin thinking about how much you can afford. You and your student will face a menu of possibilities ranging from about $10,000 per year (in-state public university) to more than $50,000 per year (expensive private college). Scholarships and financial aid may come into play, but be prepared to go without either.

Liquidate Custodial Accounts

This applies to families who will seek need-based aid, which generally can include anyone with less than about $200,000 of annual family income. Putting money in your child's name gives a tax advantage, but it is a killer for need-based aid. There are legal ways to spend down custodial accounts on behalf of your child. Speak to your lawyer or financial advisor to find out how.

Be Realistic

Your son or daughter might not get into your alma mater, but if you were applying today, you might not either.

Don't sweat it. Today's world is much more competitive, but there are also a lot more great schools today than there were thirty years ago.

Stay in the Loop about School

Keep your ear to the ground for any changes in academic performance. Grades nine and ten are typically the time when students make the lowest grades of their high school careers. A lot of them still need help getting organized and staying on top of their work.

Help Your Son or Daughter Think about Summer Activities

The days of going to summer camp—unless it is as a counselor-in-training—should now be over. Encourage your son or daughter to do something meaty. Good options include volunteering, shadowing a working professional, or even becoming a small-scale entrepreneur. If you're willing to pay for an out-of-town experience, surf www.petersons.com/highschool_home.asp?path=hs.home for a database full of ideas.

Get Informed

Your odds of getting your son or daughter to read about the college process in ninth grade are slim to none—but that doesn't mean *you* can't look ahead. For a complete overview of the college process, check out *The Fiske Guide to Getting Into the Right College*.

Understand That It's Not about You

Parents tend to assume that the path they themselves

took will also be best for their child. And though parents may clearly see how their son or daughter is influenced by peers, they often overlook how their adult peers may shape what they want from the college process. Stay tuned to your student.

"Parents who want the best for their kids continue to be overly worried about 'name' schools as opposed to wonderful schools that may be less famous. I see more and more wonderful kids, unhappy and depressed, about what is a luxury dilemma—which great college will they attend? It is a sad and worrisome trend."
—SCHOOL COUNSELOR

"It took me a while to figure out that some schools are looking for students and some have more than they need."
—SANTA CLARA UNIVERSITY MOM

✔ LEARN ABOUT HONORS, AP, AND IB COURSES

Welcome to the alphabet soup of advanced-course acronyms. Here's what you need to know:

- Many schools offer advanced courses with designations such as "honors" or "gifted and talented" (GAT). You may also see courses labeled "Pre-AP." If you're not sure how your child's school designates advanced courses, find out.

- Beginning in tenth grade at a few schools, and more commonly in grades eleven and twelve, students can take College Board Advanced Placement (AP) courses, which follow a prescribed curriculum and culminate in a nationally administered test graded on a scale of one to five. About fifteen thousand schools nationwide offer AP courses.

- At schools with both honors and AP at the same grade level, the latter are usually viewed as the most advanced. A much smaller but growing number of schools offer International Baccalaureate (IB) courses, which also follow a standard curriculum and are graded on a one to seven scale.

- Unlike AP, IB is a unified diploma program rather than simply a menu of courses. About five hundred schools across the nation offer IB.

For more information on AP and IB, head to www.apcentral.org and www.ibo.org, respectively.

HAVE FUN, VOLUNTEER

Landmark Volunteers, at www.volunteers.com, offers one- and two-week experiences at nearly sixty locations throughout the nation, many of them national parks. The program is open to students who have completed ninth grade and requires a tax-deductible contribution of $750 for a one-week experience and $1,300 for two weeks.

"Encourage a high school–age child
to look at colleges whenever the
opportunity arises, not just in the junior
and senior years. It's difficult to sort all
the information and impressions of different
campuses if the visits are concentrated
into a relatively short time span."

—YALE UNIVERSITY MOM

"If I could do it over again, I would try to fight less with my mom...but that was basically unavoidable."

VASSAR COLLEGE STUDENT

"I have had parents control the whole admissions process, and there is always resentment on the students' part."
—SCHOOL COUNSELOR

✔ A CASUAL VISIT TO HARVARD?

On a vacation to Boston, what harm can it do to swing by Harvard just to take a look? If your son or daughter is a solid B+ student, it can do *a lot* of harm (especially if the Harvard alumni magazine is on your coffee table at home). Even if your child is the top student in her class, the odds are small that she'll get in at a place that accepts less than 10 percent of the best and brightest who apply. Don't saddle a ninth grader with those expectations. If you want to see Harvard among a sample that includes Suffolk University, Northeastern, and Boston College, maybe that makes sense, assuming that you're not dragging the young one by the scruff of the neck. But if you're going to stop in at just one college, which may be a smart move at this early stage, go to Boston University or Babson. Your goal should be to stimulate interest in college campuses, not feed Ivy-League pressure.

"There are different 'feels' to schools that can only be 'felt' when visiting."

BRANDEIS UNIVERSITY STUDENT

"The official tour can be helpful, but a great thing is to go to the student center and just talk to students."

LAKE FOREST COLLEGE STUDENT

✔ CREATING YOUR OWN SMALL BUSINESS

It may seem strange to think of yourself as a business owner, but the idea is not so far-fetched. Suppose you like to baby-sit: What about creating a summer camp for younger kids in the neighborhood? Nothing fancy, just some fun activities that will allow you to take those kids off their parents' hands for a few hours each day. You'll earn some money and be the most popular teen in the neighborhood among the adult set. Mowing lawns and other outdoor chores are also obvious possibilities. And you can find a world of additional ideas on the Internet. We know a young man who made good money buying books at yard sales and then selling them on eBay. But making money is less important than the experience of being in business.

"I tell my families that they can start to visit colleges during the freshman year. If the family is going on vacation, I am more than happy to advise them on colleges near their destination that are worth visiting. I advise my students to check out the bulletin boards and newspapers to find out the issues that students are talking about."

—SCHOOL COUNSELOR

> "Good grades and high SAT scores are the worst way to get into those 'reach' schools. Excel at something unique and devote your time to that."

UNIVERSITY OF NOTRE DAME STUDENT

✔ HIGH SCHOOL BEGINS

Students

Yes, we know you won't be going to college for another four years. And no, we're not crazy. A little thinking now can pay off big-time later on. Just humor us (and your parents) for a few minutes.

Work Hard in School

Your parents have probably mentioned (once or twice) the importance of getting good grades. They may be clueless on most things, but they're right on this. Ninth grade is the first year that your grades go on your official academic transcript, which is sent to colleges when you apply.

Plan for Eleventh and Twelfth Grade

College probably seems far away right now, but it makes sense for you to be thinking about the next few years of high school. Which math course will you be taking as a senior? What about science and social studies? Are there electives that you would like to try? A plan will help you see the big picture and choose the right classes and activities.

Find a Few Activities

The things you do outside of class can be just as important as your schoolwork. Think about the activities that you like best. Are there some that you enjoy more than others? Any new ones you would like to try? With each year of high school, your life will get busier. It is better to do a few activities well than to try to do everything.

Think about Your Career

Nobody ever really knows what they want to be when they grow up, but it never hurts to think about it. In the school subject that you like best, ask the teacher if he or she has any career ideas for you. It also can't hurt to learn more about what your parents do for a living, even if you merely find out what you don't want to do. Keep an eye out for jobs that you're interested in, and think about finding a fun summer activity that might help you learn more about them.

Have Fun

Everybody needs to find a balance between work and play. People who never study are headed for trouble, but people who study too much sometimes have trouble relaxing. If you find yourself worrying about school—or college—take a break and relax. You may actually do better in school if you don't let yourself get too stressed out.

> "I wish I had tried harder on freshman and sophomore year academics. I was immature and regret the decisions I made."

Parents

✔ WHAT TO DO WITH AN UNDERACHIEVER

There is no playbook for dealing with a student who is underachieving. The fundamental issue is always whether the student lacks motivation, or whether something in the learning environment or the material itself is causing a problem.

- If you suspect real learning issues, now would be a good time to have your son or daughter tested. Sometimes a general mental health problem is the culprit, or issues with teacher(s) or peers.

- When the issue is motivation, some parents opt for an early visit to the guidance or college counselor in an effort to have someone else tell the student that, yes, grades do matter.

- Another idea is to schedule an early college visit. A peek at college life may help motivate your son or daughter.

Step two is to attend an admissions information session, where the unspoken bottom line will be "work hard or you've got no chance."

When all else fails, keep your head. Even if the light bulb doesn't go on until graduate school, it won't be the end of your student's world—or yours.

> "I wish I had understood in ninth grade that my academic performance was important."

CONNECTICUT COLLEGE STUDENT

Students

✔ YOUR HIGH SCHOOL CURRICULUM

Even outstanding students generally do not take the most academically rigorous courses in every subject, but they do so in most. In the list below, "Best Possible" assumes the most advanced courses available in each subject.

SUBJECT	BEST POSSIBLE	MINIMUM ACCEPTABLE
English	Four Years	Four Years
Social Studies	Four Years	Three Years
Math	Through Calculus AB or BC	Through Algebra II
Science	Four Years Including Biology, Chemistry, and Physics	Three Years Including Biology
Foreign Language	Four Years	Two Years
Arts	Four Years	Two Years

✔ THE IMPORTANCE OF MATH

Many schools assign students to classes based on their ability. Since math is the subject that creates the clearest distinctions among students, it typically drives these assignments. Most of the best students in math are also at or near the top in other areas as well. But some of those who are top students in other subjects are not as good in math, and these students sometimes miss out on advanced classes because of math-based tracking. If your child is in this category, pay close attention to each year's schedule and make sure that he or she is not missing opportunities in subjects outside math.

grade 10

There are no make-or-break college admissions issues in tenth grade. But smart applicants and their parents will find plenty to do. Some parental nudges are in order for procrastinating students, but parents should avoid heavy-handed pressure that might cause a backlash.

> "I started looking at colleges sophomore year, and I'm really glad I did."

SHENANDOAH UNIVERSITY STUDENT

Students
✔ COLLEGE LOOMS CLOSER

Two scenarios are possible for tenth grade. Ready to focus on college? Good! You can bet Mom and Dad are, too. Not ready to focus on college? That's okay, too, but at least stick your toe in the water.

Keep Working Hard in School

We're only reminding you of this because your parents are tired of doing it. But they're right. Your grades matter more and more each year, so if you're not working to your potential, now would be a good time to turn things around.

Take the PSAT or PLAN

The Preliminary SAT, administered once a year in mid-October, will give you practice for your real SAT. Most schools give the PSAT to students in tenth and eleventh grade. The PLAN, a pre-ACT test, is offered primarily in the South and Midwest.

Meet with College Representatives

Fall is the season when colleges send their admissions officers to high schools all over the country. Most high schools host dozens of these officers from early September through mid-November. Go to the guidance office and check out the schedule. If you have a free period or see a college that you want to know more about, go check it out and see if you can grab a minute to talk to the college representative.

Go to a College Fair

The best way to get your feet wet in the college-search game is to attend a college fair. Generally held in fall or spring, college fairs feature a few dozen—or a few hundred—college representatives standing behind tables with brochures about their schools. Fairs are an opportunity to get information and have brief conversations with admissions officers in a low-key format.

Shadow a Professional

How can a tenth grader learn about careers? It usually won't happen in school. The best way is to shadow a working professional for a day or longer, as schedules permit. If any of your parents' friends work in fields of interest to you, see if you can tag along with them during a school break. To cast a wider net, pick the brain of your guidance counselor or other adult for leads.

Apply for Cool Opportunities

If you haven't been to the guidance office yet, go there to see the possibilities for sophomores. One opportunity reserved for tenth graders is the Hugh O'Brian Youth Leadership program (www.hoby.org). The summer after tenth grade is often the first time students are eligible to apply for summer programs at colleges. See if there's a program open to high school students at a college you're interested in.

Think about Visiting Colleges

The summer after tenth grade can be a great time for low pressure visits to colleges and universities—but not if you make Mom and Dad drag you. The argument for visiting now is simple: your life is going to get a lot busier in eleventh and twelfth grade, and by doing visits now, you get ahead of the game.

Make the Most of Your Summer

You don't need to do a $5,000 program at Harvard, or spend $10,000 to save the baboons in Borneo. Do community service close to home, or get a job and take some responsibility. You can also attend summer school and lighten your load for eleventh grade. You're likely to find a better opportunity if you take the initiative in winter or early spring.

Do a Self-Evaluation

Finding yourself is the first step in finding a college. Before you start looking at schools, take a good look at yourself. Would you do best at a big college or a small one? A school in a small town or a big city? Check out our Sizing Yourself Up Survey in *The Fiske Guide to Colleges* for a complete self-evaluation tool.

"We used weekly Saturday lunches to keep track of our son's progress in an open discussion format. We tried to let him focus on his schoolwork and activities during the week."

—UNIVERSITY OF VIRGINIA DAD

"Most families should allow their kids to work through the college application process while the parents are focused on thoroughly completing the financial aid process."

—SCHOOL COUNSELOR

Students

✔ WHAT DOES PRELAW MEAN?

In a word, nothing. You can major in economics and then go to law school, or you can major in ethnomusicology and then go to law school. It makes no difference as long as you have good grades, do well on the LSAT, and submit a great application. Premed is the same way. Though you do need to take a selection of biology and chemistry courses, as well as calculus, premed is an advising program, not a major. The same cannot be said about engineering or architecture majors, which are so packed with required courses that they leave little room for electives. Majors in business are somewhere in-between: they have plenty of requirements, but offer more flexibility than those in engineering or architecture to take outside courses or do a double major. If you have even a fuzzy idea of a possible major, check it out on a college website and see what is required.

> "On a website, the colleges can show what they want to, but when you're on the campus, you can see things for yourself."

WILLIAMS COLLEGE STUDENT

 ## REGISTERING FOR THE TESTS

- Nobody signs up for standardized tests using paper forms anymore. Head to www.collegeboard.org to register for the SAT, and www.actstudent.org to register for the ACT.

- Know your test center code. Aside from your personal information, the most important thing to fill out is where you want to take the test. Each test center has a unique code, which you can look up as you register. Early registrants are the most likely to get their first choice.

- If you'd like to send your scores to colleges, have a list of them ready. (You can also save that part for later.)

- Try to complete the registration in one sitting. However, you can save your information and come back later if you choose.

- Keep in mind that at the end of the process, you'll need a credit card number to seal the deal.

✔ COLLEGE MAIL: WHERE DOES IT COME FROM?

The brochures and viewbooks that flood your mailbox come courtesy of the standardized testers. At the rate of a few cents per name, College Board and ACT sell the names and contact information of millions of students to any institution willing to pay. As you register for each of the tests, you are asked to fill out a survey that asks dozens of questions about your academic record, interests, and even your family income. If a college wants to send letters to all the students who scored above 2100 on the SAT, live in zip code 22903, are interested in science, and live in households with incomes above $100,000, the testing agencies can provide the names and addresses with a few keystrokes. To opt out of this process, either don't complete the survey or say "no" when they ask if you give permission to share your information with the colleges.

"After the PSAT, the barrage of mail and email from the colleges misleads students and even relatively sophisticated parents. Just because you get a letter from a college doesn't mean you'll get in."

—SCHOOL COUNSELOR

GET INFORMED ABOUT THE SAT SUBJECT TESTS

- Back when Mom and Dad were applying to college, these were known as Achievement tests. Only about three dozen of the nation's most selective schools require them, including the Ivy League, other private colleges like Williams and Tufts, and the University of California.

- Tests are offered in sixteen subjects. Each lasts an hour, up to three can be taken on a particular date, and it is not possible to take the SAT and a Subject Test on the same day.

- Colleges that require Subject Tests most often require two, though a few upper-crust places like Harvard and Princeton ask for three.

- Requirements aside, a good Subject Test score can be helpful at virtually any college. Since the Subject Tests measure knowledge from school classes, it generally makes sense to take them in June, at the end of a school year. Chemistry is a common choice for tenth graders, though most applicants wait until the spring of eleventh grade before starting subject tests.

- For complete information, go to www.collegeboard.org.

✔ THE MILITARY ADMISSION PROCESS

Students get out of bed early at the military academies, and students who want to apply for admission need to begin early as well. There are two gateways to information: the websites of the various academy admissions offices, and local members of Congress. Applicants must secure a nomination from the latter. Congressional offices sometimes hold information nights about the academy process and/or have information on their websites. At minimum, they will send information in response to a phone call. It is best to get started with the process early in eleventh grade. Congressional offices set their own deadlines, generally in September or October of twelfth grade.

> "The service academy applications are quite intense. Start early."

U.S. MILITARY ACADEMY STUDENT

✔ COLLEGE VISITS IN GRADE 10?

While parents are chomping at the bit to get started with the college search, the typical tenth grader is more focused on texting friends about their latest OMG moment, preparing for next week's big game, or deciding which flavor of lip gloss to wear. As the ever-practical adult, you must decide how much to rain on this parade with admonitions about college being right around the corner. It's a tough call. Your son or daughter will be ahead of the game if he or she can do some college visits by the summer of tenth grade, but the effort will be wasted if it prompts eye rolling and a sour attitude. Our advice is to be subtle. If you go to Colonial Williamsburg, do a tour of William and Mary while you're there. In New York? Take a look at Marymount Manhattan and maybe swing by NYU. Barter a little: throw in a Red Sox game if son will agree to see Boston University, or offer shopping on Magnificent Mile after seeing University of Chicago or DePaul. As always, don't fill your itinerary with only highly selective colleges. In today's climate, the first schools you think of may not be realistic, and though college may be far away, it is best to keep your expectations realistic from the start.

"Use the summer of sophomore year for casual tours, and the spring of junior year for formal visits and interviews."
—SCHOOL COUNSELOR

> "Visit colleges in your sophomore year. There's almost no time later."

PRINCETON UNIVERSITY STUDENT

✔ THE TRUTH ABOUT TEST PREP

Don't bother trying to get a definitive answer on whether paying for test prep will help your son or daughter. Some students seem to benefit from having an adult taskmaster; others do quite well on their own.

Depending on their score after preparing for the test, students will either tell you it was great (because they got a high score) or a waste of time (because they got a low score). Know that in both scenarios, the scores were probably influenced by many things other than the prep course.

Remember these two facts: the highest scoring students are the least likely to pay for test prep, and the claims of the national test prep companies about average score increases never stand up to scrutiny.

- For most students, the greatest potential gains come from familiarity with the test, and from learning a few simple strategies for how to approach it. A forty-hour course is almost guaranteed to be a waste of time, but a five- or ten-hour review might be useful.

- Students with gaps in their knowledge of the test's content, particularly in math, should consider getting a personal tutor.

- If you have a motivated student, the most sensible times for test prep are the summer after tenth grade, leading up to the PSAT in October of grade eleven; or, January to March of grade eleven, in preparation for a March or April test.

"I equate test prep courses to Weight Watchers. If you need the accountability and support system, it can be very helpful."
—SCHOOL COUNSELOR

"I took an SAT prep course that didn't help at all. After taking it, I got my lowest verbal score ever."

COLUMBIA UNIVERSITY STUDENT

"Colleges often downplay the importance of standardized test scores. In fact, test scores matter more than they say most of the time."

—SCHOOL COUNSELOR

Students

✔ THE NATIONAL MERIT PROGRAM

Most people don't know that the official name of the PSAT is PSAT/NMSQT. The latter part stands for National Merit Scholarship Qualifying Test.

Though many tenth graders take the PSAT/NMSQT, only eleventh graders are eligible for the National Merit contest.

About fifteen thousand of the top-scoring eleventh graders, or about 1.5 percent of those who take the test, are chosen as Semifinalists based on their scores. A handful of these students are weeded out because of low grades, and the rest become Finalists.

- Finalists are eligible for scholarships from three sources: National Merit itself, participating (usually large) corporations that give money to the Finalist children of their employees, and from colleges that award money to Finalists who choose to enroll.

- National Merit Finalists who go to highly selective colleges are sometimes out of luck, because most top private universities don't give money based on National Merit status.

- Many state universities, and many less-selective private ones, give Finalists a full ride. About half of all National Merit Finalists end up with some kind of award.

Students

✔ CLEAN UP YOUR EMAIL ADDRESS

It can be highly entertaining to have an email address such as sexy69@anywhere.com or dointhenasty@nowhere.com. Maybe your parents don't even know that you have it. But the joke will be on you when emails begin arriving from admissions officers at your suddenly tacky, juvenile address. Get yourself a presentable email address and keep it until you leave high school. And be sure to check it now and then. More and more colleges are sending important communication by email.

> "Standardized tests were the most demoralizing part of the process for me. I started comparing myself to my [higher-scoring] friends and looking only at the SAT and ACT ranges of the colleges. I felt horrible about my scores for a long period of time. Advice: Don't worry so much about what other people got on the tests."

BRANDEIS UNIVERSITY STUDENT

✔ THE SAT AND THE ACT: WHAT'S THE DIFFERENCE?

Students

- If you live on one of the coasts, SAT is the test you know. In the middle of the country, ACT is the test that most students take.

- Both have over a million test-takers per year, and virtually every college in the nation accepts either to fulfill its testing requirement.

■ Though the tests have a conversion chart that is designed to translate the scores of one to the other, many students believe that it is easier to score well on the ACT.

■ The latest trend, which we support, is to take both in eleventh grade and see which one suits you best.

■ The ACT is the more straightforward test and doesn't have as many wrong answers dressed up to look right as does the SAT. But the ACT often requires more knowledge of academic material. In math, for instance, you'll get trigonometry, logarithms, and matrices on the ACT but not the SAT, which has more basic math presented in trickier ways.

■ For a complete rundown on the differences between SAT and ACT, consult *The Fiske Guide to Getting Into the Right College.*

Parents

✔ BEING UNDECIDED IS OK

Back when General Motors and U.S. Steel were the titans of the American economy, students decided on a career in college and then worked until retirement in the same field. Today, U.S. Steel is long gone, GM is on life support, and students sometimes have ten careers—by their thirtieth birthday. College is a huge expense, and it makes sense to approach it with a purpose, but most eighteen-year-olds don't know what they want to do next week, let alone five years from now. In today's dynamic world, it makes no sense to ask anyone what they want to do when they grow up. How many 1995 graduates wanted careers related to the Internet? By all means, push your son or daughter to develop interests and investigate possibilities. But in the twenty-first century, being practical may mean getting a good all-around education that will prepare you for anything.

FIGURING OUT LIKES AND DISLIKES

If you're at sea about careers, consider taking the Campbell Interest and Skill Survey, which will assess your aptitude for sixty career fields. You can do it for less than twenty dollars by visiting www. profiler.com.

✔ EXPLORE CAREERS

Students

Few people plan a career; instead, it unfolds as you go from one thing you like to another. But exploring your interests today can give you a head start on tomorrow. It is never too late to change your mind, whether you're a senior in high school or a fifty-year-old.

▪ Think about What You Enjoy

A classic example is the person who likes building with blocks and ends up being an architect or engineer. If you like drawing, you may gravitate toward some kind of design. A hint: Try to separate what you're good at from what you enjoy. The latter is what you should focus on.

Read about Specific Careers
If you are intrigued by flying, ask your parents to get you a subscription to *Airliners* magazine. To learn about work in any field, jump on Wikipedia (www.wikipedia.com), where every conceivable career is profiled. You might learn something simply by googling "aerospace engineer," or any field that interests you. If all else fails, your guidance office may have a supply of career-related materials.

Talk to Working Professionals
Don't be shy if your second cousin has a really cool job. Get in touch and ask about it. Talk to your friend's mom if she has a career that sounds interesting. If you keep asking, you'll learn a lot and probably work your way into some interesting volunteer opportunities.

Create a Résumé
When you apply for a job, you need a résumé to describe what you've done in the past. Even if you're not going to start your career any time soon, a résumé helps you keep track of what you have done and gives you practice in writing about it.

Learn How Universities Are Organized
Surf a university website and click on "academics" and/ or "schools and colleges." Learn about your options. You

may find programs you had not thought of, and discover that admissions requirements vary from college to college within a university.

Learn about What You Will Study

Once you know the organizational chart of a university, dig into the details. You may think you want to study business, but what, exactly, does studying business mean? By looking up the required courses and the electives available in your areas of interest, you can put some meat on those bones.

Consider the Liberal Arts

You need not be liberal or interested in the arts to earn a liberal arts degree. The term is from hundreds of years ago when the words had different meanings than they do now. Physics is a liberal art, as is math, and some of the staunchest defenders of the liberal arts are conservative. Instead of preparing you for a particular career, studying the liberal arts teaches you to think.

Consider a Preprofessional Program

Have you known since age twelve that you wanted to study fashion design? If so, you may want to consider a school or college that specializes in fashion. You'll benefit from more hands-on opportunities in your field, but if your interests change, you may need to change schools.

Think about a Summer Program

A good way to sample college is to attend a summer program. This is especially true for those with preprofessional interests because they can use the program to try out their chosen field. If a residential program is too expensive, consider taking a course or two at a local community college.

■ Hedge Your Bets

Blinders look ridiculous on a teenager, so take them off and don't get fixated on one career or major. You may think you want to be premed, but don't pass up a neat program in the arts. If you want to be an engineer, AP English could be just the thing to set you apart from all the other applicants with only science APs.

"It was hard for me to remember all of my activities from previous years. I would advise keeping up with them as you do them."

VASSAR COLLEGE STUDENT

 ## ONE-STOP CAREER SHOPPING

You'll find video and information galore at www.mycoolcareer. com, including a self-assessment tool and thirty-minute shows on dozens of careers.

✔ PROFESSIONAL TRAINING IN THE ARTS

If you're a serious artist or musician, you'll have three options for college study: a program within a university that is related to your artistic interest, but which does not prepare you to be a professional artist; a professional art program offered within a university; or a professional art program offered by a stand-alone arts school.

We recommend that you consider all three. The first includes programs that would, for instance, prepare students interested in music to become music teachers, or focus on the business side of music. The second would give you professional training, but also offer access to the resources of a comprehensive institution. The stand-alone schools typically provide the most intense artistic experience, but also limit your options for study outside the arts.

> "I wish I had known how important my grades were earlier in my high school career."

BELLARMINE UNIVERSITY STUDENT

LEARNING ABOUT MAJORS

At www.princetonreview.com, you can read about two hundred majors, including necessary high school preparation and a sample undergraduate curriculum. From there, you can surf to colleges and universities that offer the major.

✔ KNOW THE TOP FIVE MYTHS OF COLLEGE ADMISSION

Students

5. **Students with straight As and high SAT scores should get in anywhere.** The sobering truth is that just because you stand out at your high school, it doesn't mean you'll stand out in the applicant pool of an Ivy. If you get 700s and have a 3.8 GPA, that makes you an average applicant at Dartmouth or Stanford. Being average puts your odds at 20 percent or less, and that's before considering that most admitted students have a special talent or ability that puts them over the top.

4. **Getting in is all about strategy.** Playing your cards right can help a little, but we're talking maybe 5 percent of the getting-in equation. Most college credentials can't be manufactured, and admissions officers can see through the attempts of students (and their parents) to jazz up an unexciting application.

3. **Getting in is all about pulling strings.** If only admissions officers had a nickel for every applicant whose mother has a friend whose uncle is on the board of trustees. Don't be deluded by the idea that your close family friends can peddle influence. Unless your granddad gave the school a million dollars, you're better off applying on your own merit.

2. **College admission is a crapshoot.** Admission decisions can seem random because high school students don't see the big picture. The goal of every college is to assemble a diverse and interesting class, and everybody who is admitted fills a role. The odds of admission at a particular school can change from year to year because both the pool of applicants and the college's needs change from year to year.

1. **The college admission process is fair.** Life isn't fair, either. Just because you are good enough does not mean that you'll get in. The good news? If you apply to a sensible list of colleges, your college search will be a success, even if you can't control what happens at any particular college.

"One of the most common misconceptions on the part of parents is that there are 'tricks' that will help their child get in."
—SCHOOL COUNSELOR

"Don't believe rumors about colleges you're interested in. Go there and see for yourself."

UNIVERSITY OF WISCONSIN MADISON STUDENT

FISKE'S

College Admission Pledge
for Students

I have accepted the fact that my parents are clueless. I am serene. I will betray not a tremor when they offer opinions or advice, no matter how laughable. My soul will be light as a feather when my mother elbows her way to the front of my college tour and talks the guide's ear off. I am serene.

Going to college is a stressful time for my parents, even though they are not the ones going. I recognize that neurosis is beyond anyone's control. Each week, I will calmly reassure them that I am working on my essays, have registered for my tests, am finishing my applications, have scheduled my interviews, am aware of all deadlines, and will have everything done in plenty of time. I will smile good-naturedly as my parent asks four follow-up questions at College Night.

I will try not to say "no" simply because my parents say "yes," and I will remain open to the possibility, however improbable, that they may have a point. I may not be fully conscious of my anxieties about the college search—the fear of being judged and the fear of leaving home are both strong. I don't really want to get out of here as much as I say I do, and it is easier to put off thinking about the college search than to get it done. My parents are right about the importance of being proactive, even if they do get carried away.

Though the college search belongs to me, I will listen to my parents. They know me better than anyone else, and they are the ones who will pay most of the bills. Their ideas about what will be best for me are based on years of experience in the real world. I will seriously consider what they say as I form my own opinions.

I must take charge of the college search. If I do, the nagging will stop, and everyone's anxiety will go down. My parents have given me a remarkable gift— the ability to think and do for myself. I know I can do it with a little help from Mom and Dad.

FISKE'S

College Admission Pledge
for Parents

I am resigned to the fact that my child's college search will end in disaster. I am serene. Deadlines will be missed and scholarships will be lost as my child lounges under pulsating headphones or stares transfixed at an Xbox. I am a parent and I know nothing. I am serene.

Confronted with endless procrastination, my impulse is to take control—to register for tests, plan visits, schedule interviews, and get applications. It was I who asked those four follow-up questions at College Night—I couldn't help myself. And yet I know that everything will be fine if I can summon the fortitude to relax. My child is smart, capable, and perhaps a little too accustomed to me jumping in and fixing things. I will hold back. I will drop hints and encourage, then back off. I will facilitate rather than dominate. The college search won't happen on my schedule, but it will happen.

I will not get too high or low about any facet of the college search. By doing so, I give it more importance than it really has. My child's self-worth may already be too wrapped up in getting an acceptance letter. I will attempt to lessen the fear rather than heighten it.

I will try not to say "no" simply because my son or daughter says "yes," and remain open to the possibility, however improbable, that my child has the most important things under control. I understand that my anxiety comes partly from a sense of impending loss. I can feel my child slipping away. Sometimes I hold on too tightly or let social acceptability cloud the issue of what is best.

I realize that my child is almost ready to go and that a little rebellion at this time of life can be a good thing. I will respect and encourage independence, even if some of it is expressed as resentment toward me. I will make suggestions with care and try to avoid unnecessary confrontation.

Paying for college is my responsibility. I will take a major role in the search for financial aid and scholarships and speak honestly to my child about the financial realities we face.

I must help my son or daughter take charge of the college search. I will try to support without smothering, encourage without annoying, and consult without controlling. The college search is too big to be handled alone—I will be there every step of the way.

grade 11

Fall of grade eleven is still relatively relaxed. Aside from the PSAT, which comes in mid-October, there are few crucial dates. The spring is a different story: SAT and ACT dates come fast and furious, college visits should be a priority for spring break, and students should have a working list of college possibilities by summer.

> "Students are applying earlier across the board. Rolling admissions colleges are filling up before January."
> —SCHOOL COUNSELOR

✔ ACADEMICS

Students

Strap on your helmet. Junior year is when everything hits the fan. Work hard, be a leader, and have fun.

■ **Enroll in Tough Courses**

This is the year to challenge yourself. As a senior, you'll be waist-deep in college applications. Now is when you can take an AP course and actually get the score in time to put it on your college application. Remember, if you apply early decision or early action, your junior grades will be the last ones the admissions offices see.

Get to Know Your Teachers

If talking to your teachers doesn't come naturally, make an effort. Linger after class to discuss the lesson. Come in during a free period to chat about a class topic. The teacher will look at you through new eyes—and will be more likely to give you a good grade or write you a glowing letter of recommendation. Plus, you might actually learn something.

Participate in Class

Most students think that grades are the bottom line in school. They are, for the most part, but when it comes time for teachers to write letters of recommendation, grades are often less important than how much you have contributed to class. Do yourself a favor and speak up.

Save Your Best Work

Your teachers know you, but when it comes time for them to write recommendations, they may have trouble remembering the specifics of your best work (having graded hundreds of papers and all). Save your best stuff, and if you ask a teacher to write a recommendation for you, arm him or her with the specifics necessary to do a great job.

Think about Your College Essays

In the spring, many eleventh-grade English classes focus on the personal essay. If yours does, work hard and you'll save yourself a lot of grief in the fall of twelfth grade. If not, think about what to write. Ask a teacher or counselor to help you brainstorm.

"I started visiting schools in the spring of junior year, and took the SAT in January of junior year. I recommend this path. I don't think I would have been ready to seriously consider a school before this point."

BROWN UNIVERSITY STUDENT

"Stay out of trouble so you don't have to check yes to suspensions. It's embarrassing."

PURDUE UNIVERSITY STUDENT

✔ STANDARDIZED TESTING, GRADE 11

We know you hate this part, but avoidance only prolongs the agony. If you get on top of your standardized testing now, most of it will be done by the end of eleventh grade.

■ Take the PSAT (Again)

It's still just practice unless you are one of those 99th percentile people who might qualify for the National Merit Scholarship contest. If you think National Merit recognition is a possibility, do some practice tests to get comfortable before you take it.

■ Analyze How You Did

The PSAT is in October, and results should be back by early December. Use them to assess your strengths and weaknesses in preparation for taking the SAT after New Year's. Don't be too concerned with a low score: The PSAT is shorter and not always an accurate predictor of your score on the SAT.

■ Prepare for the SAT or ACT

Carve out a little time during winter break, or in January, to take a close look at one or both tests. Depending on your school's calendar, you may have spring break for a little review. If you are thinking about getting a tutor or taking a prep class, ask about the qualifications and experience of the person who will be teaching you.

Choose Your Test Dates

Most students take their first SAT in March or May, and their first ACT in April. For early birds, or those with scheduling conflicts in the spring, January is an option for the SAT and February for the ACT. If you're applying to highly selective schools, pencil in the SAT Subject Tests for June.

Register for the Tests

Many teens procrastinate when it comes time to register for standardized tests. Fact: the longer you wait, the less likely that you will get your preferred test site if there are space issues. Fact: If you miss the deadline, which is about thirty-five days before each test date, you'll have to pay a $25 fee for late registration.

Get Questions and Answers

Your first time taking the test will probably not be your last, so when you register, pay extra to get copies of the test questions and your answers. You'll have a much clearer idea of why you scored as you did, and how to prepare for the next time.

Survive Test Day

Too many students stay up until the wee hours on Friday night and expect to do well Saturday morning on the SAT. Treat it like a normal school night, and if you don't know exactly where the test site is located, leave a few minutes early. Don't forget your ID, pencils, a calculator, a snack, and a watch.

Do It All Again

If you're fairly certain that you want to apply early decision or early action, consider taking the SAT or ACT twice during your junior year. Two scores before the summer break will give you a clear idea of where you stand as you weigh your options. The next test may not be until October.

Consider SAT Subject Tests

Now is the logical time to take tests in courses that you are finishing, such as Math Level II (at the end of precalculus), Math Level I (Algebra II), foreign language, history, or science. Take three if you are required to do so and think you can handle it, but if you want to prepare, limiting yourself to two on a single test date is probably the wise choice.

See How Your Scores Compare

Take a look at the score profiles of the colleges you are interested in. If you match the scores of accepted students at a school that takes more than 50 percent of its applicants, you have an excellent chance. If you match the averages at Yale, you probably have about a 15–20 percent chance.

FREE TEST PREP

The price is right at www.number2.com, where students can access free test-prep tutorials for SAT and ACT that adapt to the students' abilities.

"Take both the SAT and ACT early, then decide which is easier and take only that one."

KENYON COLLEGE STUDENT

"While SAT tutors are expensive, if you can afford it, I suggest getting one. The only reason is that if you have someone with authority telling you to study for the test, the practicing becomes homework, thus having the same priority as your schoolwork."

WILLIAMS COLLEGE STUDENT

✔ THE COLLEGE SEARCH, GRADE 11

This year starts at a leisurely pace. But after junior college night, usually in mid-winter, things will start moving faster.

■ Size Yourself Up

Even if you took our advice to do a self-assessment in tenth grade—and we doubt you did—take another look at your likes and dislikes. Do you value one-on-one interaction with your teachers? Think small. Are you looking for a specialized major? Maybe a large school would be best. For a complete rundown on the various options, check out *The Fiske Guide to Getting Into the Right College*.

■ See Ten College Representatives

Keep an eye on the list of visiting admissions officers who will start showing up at your school beginning in late August. Be sure to fill out an inquiry card with every representative you see. If you're the only one in attendance, use the visit as an impromptu personal interview. Meeting with a college representative can help you evaluate whether a visit to campus would be useful, and it's good practice for an interview later on.

■ Work the College Fairs

If you floated noncommittally around the college fair last year, treat it like speed dating this time. The guidance office will probably have a list of the participating colleges, and it's likely that some of the same representatives that came to your school will also be at the fair. The more times you check in with them and ask questions, the more likely that the representative will begin to remember you and your interest.

Do an Online Search

You'll find search programs at dozens of websites, but we recommend that you go to www.collegeboard.org and click on "find a college." There you can make choices about size, location, selectivity, etc., and generate a list of colleges that fit your criteria. Keep narrowing it down until you get a manageable list of possibilities.

Surf the Web

You can dig up almost anything online. Visit the site of the college newspaper, see what you can find on Facebook, and browse the blogs on each school's official website. Find out if your high school subscribes to Naviance, a Web-based tool for students and parents that offers a wealth of other information.

See Your Guidance Counselor

Your counselor can help you generate a list of possible options, or at least point you to some resources that will help. Many counselors keep records of where past applicants have been accepted to help you gauge where you might get in.

Do Spring-Break Visits

Believe it or not, spring break of grade eleven is one of the last times that you can visit colleges while you are on break and they are in session. A visit while the students are on campus will give you a more accurate feel for what life might be like. The colleges are empty in the summer and your life will be stressful in the fall of grade twelve.

Learn Where Older Friends Are Going

In mid-December, and again in April, your high school will be abuzz with news of where the seniors have gotten in. Pay attention to the college choices of seniors whom you respect. Quiz them about why they made the choices they did, as well as what they think of the places you are considering.

Think about Reaches and Safe Schools

Nobody has any trouble finding dream schools, which are typically selective and therefore called "reaches." More important is to find some colleges that you like and where you are also fairly certain that you will be admitted. Be sure to include one or two in the mix that your parents can definitely pay for.

Narrow It Down to Ten by Summer

This is a goal, not a requirement. But the main problem for many applicants is narrowing it down. There's no way you can consider twenty schools and visit them all. But you can visit eight or ten with a little planning. If one of your favorites is not hugely selective, there is no need to consider applying to more than half a dozen.

> "A common myth is that you will fall in love instantly with the college that is right for you."

UNIVERSITY OF PENNSYLVANIA STUDENT

"I tell the students to think about what they need to be happy. Vegan food? A practice room for piano? A place to worship? The ability to participate in theater if majoring in something else? I ask them to come up with the six criteria they need to be happy across all aspects of their life—and then explore all of these facets at each school."

—SCHOOL COUNSELOR

✔ COLLEGES THAT COUNT CONTACTS

Students

If you're the type of person who hangs back and lets your parents make all the arrangements for visits, call the admissions offices, etc., you should know that the colleges are spying on you. Many of the small colleges record every contact, whether it is from you or your parents. The times that you make contact allow you to demonstrate that you are interested, and therefore likely to enroll if admitted (which, in turn, makes admission more likely). If Mom is always the one making contact, schools may wonder about how serious your interest really is, and how well you can function on your own.

"We (parents) were advised by our guidance counselor not to call the colleges if we had any general questions and instead have the student call the admissions offices at various universities."
—WASHINGTON UNIVERSITY IN ST. LOUIS MOM

✔ FIND OUT THE COST OF A YEAR

Parents

Few things are worse than being blindsided by the cost of a year at your son or daughter's first-choice college.

☐ Look up the costs of the various options.

☐ Beginning in eleventh grade, set parameters for the college search and discuss these with your son or daughter.

- Remember that scholarships and/or financial aid are never guaranteed, and if they will be necessary in order for your child to attend particular schools, say so now.

- Prepare yourself. Even for people who think they have kept up with the cost of college, the numbers can be eye-opening.

"'Demonstrated interest' can be a factor at small liberal arts institutions. At St. Lawrence University, the admissions folks use it to see how well the students know SLU."
—SCHOOL COUNSELOR

"Set a dollar amount ahead of time for what you're willing to contribute to set the student's expectations for what is really affordable. Get the student involved in the Expected Family Contribution formula, and make it clear that since they are a part of the family they will be expected to contribute to the EFC."
—CHAPMAN UNIVERSITY MOM

✔ THE COLLEGE SEARCH DON'T LIST

Any one of the following five blunders can put a crimp in your college search.

Don't Get Your Heart Set on One College

There are probably dozens, if not hundreds, of colleges where you could thrive. The frenzy of the college search is about getting into big name schools. But once you get beyond the name, little is unique about any particular place. You can always find another good one that shares the same traits.

Don't Get Fooled by Phony "Honors"

Have you heard yet from "Who's Who among American High School Students?" Or the National Youth Leadership Forum? If so, don't think for a minute that you are being honored for anything real. These and other organizations sell products you can buy, not honors you have won.

Don't Obsess Over the Rankings

Have you memorized the first tier of the *U.S. News & World Report* rankings? We hope not. The rankings are a reasonably good indicator of the prestige of various colleges, but they say little about where you would be happy. And besides, the rankings change every year for no obvious reason other than selling magazines.

Don't Pick Colleges to Impress Your Friends

Some people do the college search vicariously through their friends. Instead of finding colleges they like, these people simply apply to all the places their friends are looking at. The right college for a friend isn't necessarily the right one for you.

Don't Worry Too Much about the Weather

The cold hard truth is that most of the nation's best colleges are located where the weather gets chilly in the winter. Is the weather really that big a deal? If you want to pick a place to live based on the weather, wait until you are ready to pick a nursing home.

"Don't apply to places just because your friends are."

LAWRENCE UNIVERSITY STUDENT

"Be open-minded to schools far from home."

UNIVERSITY OF MARY WASHINGTON STUDENT

> "If you want to go to Harvard to say you are going to Harvard, you're going for the wrong reason."

VASSAR COLLEGE STUDENT

✔ THE COLLEGE SEARCH, GRADE 11

Even the most engaged eleventh grader can seem like a procrastinator to motivated parents. Easy there, Mom. The college search will never happen as fast as you want it to, but it will happen.

Learn When to Push and When to Pull Back

It's one of the hardest things about parenting: when to give an extra push, and when to understand that a teenager needs to do it under his own power. The right answer can change from day to day and week to week. Find a balance.

Adjust to Today's Admissions Climate

Twenty-five years ago, Yale accepted 20 percent of its applicants and everyone thought it was tough to get admitted. Today, Yale accepts 9 percent from a better applicant pool, and the same increase in selectivity is being played out all over the country. Be open to the schools you have never heard of that might be right for your son or daughter. The flip side of rising selectivity is that there are now more colleges where your child would be happy and get a first-class education.

Set Financial Parameters

It was once considered bad form to tell a student that he or she could not go to particular colleges because of cost. The world is different today, and parents should not be shy about setting limits on the amount that can be spent. But don't eliminate particular colleges until after the aid offers come in.

Help Research Colleges

If you learned generalities about the admissions process last year, get into the specifics now. We recommend that you search on parallel lines with your son or daughter. Know the basics of what he or she is interested in, and take a look for yourself. Try not to speak too often unless you are spoken to.

Set Up a Filing System

To kids raised in the digital age, paper files are an alien concept. But the mailbox will still collect missives from the colleges on a daily basis, and at least some of them will be worth keeping. Paper copies of things like test scores, report cards, and aid awards should be filed.

Keep an Eye on Test Registration

This is your son or daughter's responsibility, but you should be looking over his or her shoulder. Test registration is the deadline most frequently missed in the spring of grade eleven. Since you're the one who pays the late fees, don't be shy about giving an extra nudge.

Help Arrange College Visits

Most of the planning for college visits can now be done on the colleges' websites, making it more likely that your son or daughter will take the initiative. Encourage him or her to go beyond the standard tour/information session and inquire about sitting in on classes, talking with professors, and staying overnight in the dorms.

Be a Sounding Board

If you nag too much, your teen will stop confiding in you. Have patience and she'll eventually talk to you, and maybe even ask your opinion. Remember that your role is not to answer her questions, but to help her find her own answers.

Do an Estimate of Aid Eligibility

Several sites allow parents to anonymously enter their financial information and get an estimate of their ability to qualify for need-based aid. We recommend the College Board website (www.collegeboard.com/student/pay/add-it-up/401.html). The estimate should be used as a ballpark figure and doesn't mean that you'll actually get aid (just that you'll need it).

"Our daughter initially delayed her search as though in a self-induced state of denial. Once we visited several schools, she zeroed in on one she really liked. The rest, except for a few tears, was relatively easy."

—DUKE UNIVERSITY MOM

"Students are often more realistic than the parents, who sometimes operate as if the world has not changed in twenty-five years."

—SCHOOL COUNSELOR

✔ KNOW THE FACTS ABOUT ATHLETICS AND ADMISSIONS

The trickiest shell game of all is the search for athletic scholarships.

- The sad truth: Outside of football and basketball, there is not much money available. Even in Division I, many of the very best players must settle for partial scholarships. And don't underestimate the level of competition in Division III, which is far stiffer than many people realize.

Money aside, being a recruited athlete can mean a boost in a student's admission chances, but the process starts early. Students should contact college coaches with a one-page letter or email by spring of eleventh grade.

Depending on the sport, students should also send an athletics résumé, an endorsement from a high school or club coach, and/or a video of themselves playing. Mom and Dad inevitably do much of the associated legwork.

In some sports, summer camps are where the coaches look for promising players.

Keep in mind that for every ten players in whom a coach expresses interest, only one may end up getting a scholarship. If you're a soccer goalie, your chances of getting a scholarship may depend on where the other highly recruited goalies, who may be just a bit taller or quicker than you are, decide to enroll.

No matter how encouraging a coach may be, never count on a scholarship until you see the offer in black and white.

"Create a folder for all of the documents that are needed for each school's application. It is easy to lose track of passwords and PINs."

—HARVARD UNIVERSITY DAD

"I arranged all college visits, organized all paperwork, and kept track of dates and deadlines."

—COLORADO STATE UNIVERSITY MOM

✔ THE COLLEGE SEARCH DON'T LIST

There are fifty ways to leave your lover and five hundred ways that overzealous parents can hamstring a college search. Here are a few:

Don't Live through Your Son or Daughter
Parents talk among themselves about the college search long before students have a clue. Unfortunately, parents

can confuse what their friends think—or what will impress their friends—with what is best for their son or daughter. Let your child start with a clean slate.

Don't Overemphasize College Choice
It is not the most important decision in anyone's life. For students who do an intelligent search and assemble good options, the final decision isn't significant at all. Success in life has less to do with where you go to college than who you are and what you do.

Don't Dismiss Colleges You've Never Heard Of
Counselors try to convince students that the most famous colleges are not necessarily the best for them, but sometimes parents are an even tougher sell. Many excellent small colleges are unknown to the general public because they don't have big-time sports teams, but the small colleges often have exemplary reputations among those who know higher education (including graduate school admissions offices).

Don't Be an Enabler
Many students are passive because they know that eventually Mom or Dad will step in. If Mom and Dad stop doing so, a few things will slip through the cracks at first, but once a student realizes that he or she is the responsible one, fewer balls will drop. Better to establish the new pattern now than to wait until next year.

Don't Lose Patience

Waiting for a teen to take control can be like water torture. Every parent gets frustrated now and then, but try to minimize the number of times you do so. The true test of the college search is not the end result, but whether you and your son or daughter can get through it on reasonably good terms.

> "Too many parents speak for their kids, ask all the questions, do the applications, and mess up the essays."
> —SCHOOL COUNSELOR

> "Parents need to relax. Constant reminders only frustrate the student."

DARTMOUTH COLLEGE STUDENT

> "Parents are the chauffeur, banker, and sounding board throughout the process."
> —SCHOOL COUNSELOR

✔ MAKING THE MOST OF COLLEGE VISITS

Students

Visits are a crucial part of the college search—and among the most stressful. In addition to looking at the schools, you'll probably be at close quarters with Mom and Dad. Take a deep breath and do the following:

Have a Plan
Don't just show up and gawk. What are you going to look for on campus? Would it help to make a list? Have a systematic way of recording your impressions when they're fresh. And once you've established your criteria, look for the same things everywhere you go.

Arrange the Visits Yourself
Most of the arranging can be done on the colleges' websites. There, you'll find a schedule of tours and information sessions, the two primary staples. If advance registration is required, you can do it there. Most schools have a list of nearby hotels posted, and a few even have driving directions to other nearby institutions.

Avoid College Breaks

Check the academic schedule of the colleges before you make plans, and try to catch them when classes are in session. The best day to visit is often a Friday because you can sample academic life in the morning and weekend life in the evening.

Get Interviews Where Possible

Interviews are a way of showing interest, which almost always helps you. Before you go, think of a topic or two about which you would be comfortable talking for ten or fifteen minutes. Most interviewers will let you take the conversation toward one of your interests.

Don't Sweat the Interview

The goal is simply to have a conversation. The admissions officer will be trying just as hard as you are to make a good impression. If you're nervous and tongue-tied, no one will hold it against you. (They'll be flattered that you care enough to be tongue-tied.)

Sit In on a Class, See a Prof

One possibility is to pick a particular class that you're interested in, such as introductory biology, and visit it at each of the colleges on your list as a basis of comparison. Some colleges have professors in every department who are designated to talk with prospective students. If not, check to see if any professors have office hours on the day you visit.

Ask about Overnights

The thought of staying overnight in a dorm can be intimidating for an eleventh grader. If you're not ready, don't sweat it, but rest assured that any student who signs up as a host will take good care of you. Be aware that some schools offer overnights only to seniors.

Cut Loose on Your Own

Whether or not you stay overnight, be sure to get time on your own. The tour guide will be repeating the college's standard PR line. Other students are likely to be more candid. Find the places where students relax and watch them interact.

See No More Than Two Schools Per Day

If you try to cram three visits into one day, you'll end up tired, late, and stressed. It is far better to take your time. When planning your itinerary, remember that you'll probably get lost once or twice. If you have an interview, plan on arriving early to make sure you're on time.

Clarify What You Want

At this stage, it is not important to identify a particular school, but it would be helpful to settle on the type of institution you want. Some students remain undecided throughout and apply to a variety of types, but if you can narrow it down, your life will be much simpler.

"Study the website before the visit to get an idea of what you want to look at."

HARVARD UNIVERSITY STUDENT

"Prepare a list of questions before you visit and don't be afraid to ask all of them."

VASSAR COLLEGE STUDENT

"Visit all of your potential colleges early and visit your top schools at least twice."

GEORGIA TECH STUDENT

"Interviews were not as serious and important as I expected."

COLGATE UNIVERSITY STUDENT

"I encourage students with a strong academic interest to contact college faculty. Our students who have done this always gain a wonderful wealth of information and can convey to the admissions office that they have been in contact with Professor 'so and so.'"
—SCHOOL COUNSELOR

✔ A QUESTION FOR THE INTERVIEW

An interview is not an inquisition, but you should still be prepared for two possible questions. The first, not used as much as it once was, is: "Have you read any good books lately?" Think of a book, preferably one that you have read outside of class, that you would be comfortable talking about. Second, you're almost guaranteed to be asked if you yourself have any questions. Think about it before you arrive. A good question is one that isn't answered on the college's website. Our favorite: How does your college differ from other similar institutions? Feel free to cite the names of competitor colleges if you have your choices narrowed down. Without disparaging the competition, the admissions officer ought to be able to tell you why students choose his or her institution.

✔ KEEP AWAY FROM INTERVIEWS

The flood of applications to selective colleges has put interviews on the endangered list. With some exceptions, only small colleges now offer them on campus. If your teen is having an interview, we recommend that you deliver him or her to the admissions office, preferably a few minutes early, and then take a hike. Go on a tour, wander around on your own, get a bite to eat in the student center, etc. Under the pressure of an interview, any teen is likely to be self-conscious with Mom and Dad around, and unsavory family dynamics have a way of asserting themselves at awkward times. Give your child some space and connect again when the pressure is off.

✔ COLLEGE VISIT DON'T LIST

Students

You'll be in unfamiliar territory and a little stressed. Try to avoid the following mishaps:

Don't Be Late

There are few worse feelings than being late for an interview. You'll be lost, straining to see signs for the admissions office, and frantically asking directions from passersby. Sound like fun? After this harrowing experience, your odds of enjoying the visit will be low.

Don't Be Intimidated

You and your parents are about to buy a product that will cost anywhere from $50,000 to $250,000 over four years. Kick the tires and look under the hood. It is natural for you to focus on impressing the admissions office, but it is also the college's job to impress you.

Don't Have Knee-Jerk Reactions

So what if the tour guide is not your favorite person? Or if the first two students you see look like geeks? Try to get the big picture while not being too swayed by little things which, though they are worth noting, may not have real significance. And try not to hate a school just because you visit on a rainy day.

■ Don't Treat Your Parents Like Dirt

You would be amazed at how many students have cringe-inducing conversations with their parents as admissions officers look on in horror...Don't take out your anxiety on Mom and Dad. If you're accustomed to addressing your mother like a servant, it is best not to advertise that fact.

"After you go to the information session, talk with the admissions officer and ask a question. Even if you think you have all of the information you need, make one up. Ask for their business card and follow through with the contact. Tell them about your interest in the college."

COLLEGE OF WILLIAM AND MARY STUDENT

> "Don't believe the myth that college admissions officers will haze you during the interview."

GEORGE WASHINGTON UNIVERSITY STUDENT

✔ THE SUMMER AFTER GRADE 11

Students

The items below are options (after the first one, which is mandatory). There are many great ways to spend your summer:

Take a Break

This is a no-brainer for most people, but too many of today's students go straight from school exams to the ACT to summer school to college visits. We think everyone should take a break. The fall of senior year will be no picnic; do what is necessary to be fresh when it begins.

Do Community Service

It is not necessary to travel halfway around the world to serve others. If you need ideas, check in with the guidance office, your church, or your local United Way. Use the time to step out of your normal surroundings and learn about a different slice of life.

Do Volunteer Work

Instead of flipping burgers, be open to more substantive work, even if you don't get paid. Build a website for someone, volunteer to assist at a veterinarian's office, or work on a political campaign. If you're lucky, volunteer work can evolve into a paid position.

Earn Some Money

Work is perfectly honorable, though unless money is a household concern, we recommend emphasizing the experience you'll get rather than merely making a buck with a menial job. Any job that requires you to work with customers is good experience.

Be an Entrepreneur

Nothing is more impressive than earning money with your own idea. It can be as simple as setting up a babysitting service or as complex as configuring computer hard drives. Going into business for yourself takes some planning, but you don't need to make a pile of money for the experience to be worthwhile.

Do a College Summer Program

The variety of available programs is truly staggering. We recommend that you take subjects that you might not otherwise have access to, like an introduction to engineering or a program in film-making. For a good searchable list of programs, head to www.petersons.com.

Be a Camp Counselor

This is a time-honored option for teens, especially those who attended a camp when they were younger. The main prerequisite is a desire to work with younger kids. Be aware that working at a camp is a lot more work and a lot less fun than being a camper.

Do a Service Trip

There will be a need for volunteers on the Gulf Coast for the foreseeable future, and most inner-city schools and programs always appreciate a helping hand. Service trips are also available to almost any corner of the globe. The latter can be expensive but well worth it for those who have the money.

Visit Colleges

A visit in the summer is not as good as one during the school year, but who has time to do all their visits during school? The busiest time on college campuses, indeed, is early August (a good reason to consider June if you have the choice). If you like a school that you see in the summer, consider visiting again in the spring if you are accepted.

Work on Your College Essay

The fall of your senior year will be frantic from the first day of school until the beginning of winter break. Summer is the time when you can collect your thoughts and focus on your essay. Even if you do only a rough draft, you'll have a head start in the fall when you write the real thing.

"I wish I had written my college essays in the summer."

COLUMBIA UNIVERSITY STUDENT

"Parents should force their kids to complete college essays in the summer."

STANFORD UNIVERSITY STUDENT

 A SOURCE FOR SUMMER ADVENTURES

If you want to hit the road to an exotic destination with the possibility of making some money or performing service, check out www.backdoorjobs.com, a place to find "short-term job adventures."

✔ PAYING FOR A PRICY SUMMER PROGRAM?

The array of summer opportunities for high school students may sound wonderful—until you see the price tag. Summer programs at colleges, and other faraway opportunities, average about $1,500 per week. Are they worth it? Maybe. If the student is motivated and will use the time to sample college life, study a subject of interest, and/or have a personal growth experience, it could be life-changing. If the angle is to pad the college résumé, or if the lure is a so-called "honor," then the program is unlikely to deliver the advertised benefit. Most programs will admit any student who applies on time, has a decent academic record, and can pay the bill. That goes for Harvard Summer School on down to the most humble program. Spending a summer at a particular college will usually do very little to help a student get in at that college, though it could help her decide if she wants to go.

"The stress I stuck myself with was the hardest thing about the college search."

ROLLINS COLLEGE STUDENT

grade 12

For students, the fall of senior year is likely to be the most frenetic of their young lives. It is a challenge to keep pace with demanding schoolwork while simultaneously managing the college process, playing sports, etc. Mom and Dad can help make sure that details are not overlooked. By mid-February, the skies will clear.

> "Go for your reaches!!! You never know."

UNIVERSITY OF BRITISH COLUMBIA STUDENT

Students

✔ STANDARDIZED TESTING, GRADE 12

By late fall, you can finally put standardized tests in the rearview mirror. But for now, stay focused.

Review Testing Requirements at Colleges

Take a serious look at which tests are required by which institutions. If you've added a highly selective school to your list, be sure you are not surprised by a Subject Test requirement.

Plan Your Senior-Year Testing Schedule

Unless you live in one of the nineteen states that offers a September ACT, October will be the first time you can test during your senior year. Scores from October should be in time for consideration if you are applying early decision or early action.

Designate Colleges to Receive Scores

For the SAT, send the scores with your highest mark on each of the three sections, and if applicable, your Subject Test scores. For ACT, send your highest composite score, and if you had a significantly higher section score on a test with a lower or equal composite, send that, too.

Consider Test-Score Optional Schools

A critical mass of small colleges, and a handful of universities, now offer the opportunity to apply without sending an SAT or ACT score. The list includes mainly progressive-leaning liberal arts colleges, but more traditional institutions such as Holy Cross, Wake Forest, and Union are also on the list.

Review Scores Required for Scholarships

Colleges almost never specify a required test score for admission, but they often do for scholarships. Fifty points on the SAT or one point on the ACT can translate directly into cash. If your scores place you close to a scholarship cutoff, it may make sense to take the test one more time in January or February.

"I did much better on the ACT than the SAT."

—UNIVERSITY OF VERMONT STUDENT

"Bring snacks to the SAT."

JOHNSON AND WALES UNIVERSITY STUDENT

> "My SAT score converted to the ACT scale was about five points lower than my highest ACT. That makes a huge difference."

UNIVERSITY OF FLORIDA STUDENT

✔ *Students* GETTING TEACHER RECOMMENDATIONS

Procrastination often strikes students who are asking for teacher recommendations. Don't be shy. The teachers know you'll be coming. The greatest sin is to wait until the last minute.

☐ Choose Teachers Carefully

Don't pick the teacher who gave you an easy "A." Instead, go for the ones who know you best, or for whom you worked hardest, or for whom you did your best work. Check the requirements of your colleges before you ask; you may only need one. Be sure to apprise the teachers of your first application deadline.

Ask Your Teachers Soon

Mid-September is a good time. If you want to wait a little longer as you are getting to know a twelfth-grade teacher, that's fine. Keep in mind that popular teachers may have twenty kids who ask them for letters. It's better to be the first to ask than the twentieth.

Give Teachers Your Résumé and Best Work

Remember when we told you to save your best work? Now is the time to dig up the stuff from classes you took with the teachers whom you have asked to write recommendations. A résumé may jog their memories about your involvements outside of class.

Follow Up with Your Teachers (Politely)

About a week before your first application deadline, follow up with your teachers. Say something like, "Just wanted you to know that I am sending in my application(s)" or "Just wanted to make sure that you have everything you need." They'll thank you and maybe even happily tell you that they have sent it.

Get an Additional Letter?

Too many students ask for too many letters of recommendation. An extra one doesn't help except in the unlikely event that the person can say something that your other recommenders cannot. A letter from a big-shot friend of the family who barely knows you but is an alum of First Choice U. will be worthless.

✔ CAN I ASK MY ART TEACHER?

The teacher you know best may be your art teacher or the yearbook sponsor, and it is natural to wonder if a letter from someone like that would be helpful. The answer is generally "no." In almost every case, recommendation letters should come from teachers in English, social studies, math, science, or foreign language, with the best combination (where two are required) being one from an English teacher and one from a math or science teacher.

"Get your name on all those lists that the colleges track—the tour, info session, visits to your school, college fairs, etc."

UNIVERSITY OF NOTRE DAME STUDENT

"I recommend that everyone apply early action somewhere, even if you don't know where you want to go. It forces you to write your essays and get your recommendations."

NORTHWESTERN UNIVERSITY STUDENT

"It's bad luck to wear a t-shirt from a college you applied to before you get in."

HOWARD UNIVERSITY STUDENT

✔ EARLY DECISION AND EARLY ACTION

If your college search is on schedule, consider applying early. But be mindful of the different rules that apply to the various programs:

▢ Understand the Requirements

With early decision (ED), you make a commitment to enroll if admitted. In most cases, early action (EA) leaves you free to apply anywhere else under any plan and to wait until May 1 to decide if you will attend. A few colleges, such as Yale and Stanford, use "restrictive" early action, which prevents you from filing other early applications but still allows you to accept or decline if admitted.

▢ Don't "Apply ED Somewhere"

Applying ED closes off options. If you're admitted, you go. You don't get to weigh offers from other colleges, and you have no basis for asking to get additional aid. ED generally makes sense only when you want to give yourself an advantage at a reach school where you would definitely go if admitted.

▢ Send Your Scores Pronto

The approach of an early deadline often sets off a mad scramble to send standardized-test scores, especially for students who want to wait and see their October scores before deciding what to send. If you are in this category, you'll almost certainly need to rush your scores once the October ones come in.

Consider a Quickie Visit

If you're thinking about applying ED—maybe to a place you visited in the summer—it often makes sense to do a quick October visit to make sure the choice is a good one. If it's EA, the visit can wait.

Make Sure Your Counselor Signs Off

For ED, your counselor will usually need to sign your application testifying that he or she has made you aware of the requirement to enroll if admitted. If you try to weasel your way out of an ED commitment, it makes your high school look bad.

Students

✔ THE COLLEGE SEARCH, GRADE 12

Things are getting serious. The following are to-dos for your applications:

Narrow Down Your List

If you don't do it now, you'll pay later. Some applicants punt and apply to, say, twelve colleges. After all the stress of applying to that many schools, these applicants often get in at eight or nine. More stress. Nobody can attend more than one school, and it is often hard to decide among a fistful of offers in April.

Review Your School Transcript

In September or October, ask your counselor to give you an unofficial copy of your transcript. Make sure your personal information is correct—especially your Social Security number—and double-check that none of your courses have been left out and that your grades are accurate.

Register on the Colleges' Websites

Click on "apply" and check out the application you'll be required to complete. Take a close look at all the questions you'll need to answer, especially the essays. Also note whether you will be asked to self-report your grades (as at the Universities of California and Washington, among others).

Review the Common Application and Supplements

Many applicants will already be familiar with the Common App and its menu of essay questions. But some get tripped up by the supplements, which consist of questions that vary from school to school. In a few cases, such as the University of Chicago, the supplement is as hard as the application itself.

Get Necessary Information from Parents

If you're applying through the Web, which we recommend, you'll need a credit card to pay the application fee. You'll need to know the degrees that your parents earned, when they got them, and where. Get your graduation date, your school code, and relevant contact information from your counselor.

Finish Your Essays

Or should we say, "Start your essays"? If you haven't found the time yet, force yourself to get started. If you've got writer's block, start with a free-form brainstorm to find your topic: write down literally anything that comes to mind and narrow the list down later. Once you have a topic, write a stream of consciousness draft. Then put it aside for a few days and come back with fresh eyes.

Do an Activity Chart

Take a look at the chart in the Common Application and/or any other applications you will complete. List anything for which you got paid in the section for Work Experience. You may need to consult Mom or Dad about your academic honors going back to ninth grade. Try not to forget anything.

Proofread Everything

This may be obvious, but proofing is much harder when you're stressed. Many, many applications include glaring errors that students would never make on ordinary assignments. Take your time, check your facts, and let others help you look for mistakes.

Go Online, Fill Out, Send

We recommend that you work on your applications off-line for the most part, then open the site to cut and paste or transcribe information from a piece of paper. After you've done the real work, make sure you don't get tripped up by all the screens to click through before sending. If an email acknowledgment does not appear, you'll need to investigate.

Follow Up on Colleges' Websites

Once you have sent your application, you can usually track its progress on the college websites after you log in. Don't panic if the first thing you see is a note that the college has not received your transcript and recommendations. These may take a few more days, especially if they are sent through the mail.

"I started the Common Application in September and worked on it steadily until November."

UNIVERSITY OF DENVER STUDENT

"Always have your counselor or parents check the application before you send it."

BELOIT COLLEGE STUDENT

> "While filling out applications, have a sheet with facts such as your Social Security number and parent information. It becomes extremely tedious having to search for that."

SOUTHERN METHODIST UNIVERSITY STUDENT

✔ THE APPLICATION DON'T LIST

Students

The following are common pitfalls. Some are worse than others, but all will cause you unnecessary stress and may harm your chances.

Don't Have an Itchy "Send" Finger

Yes, we know the pressure is unbearable. We know how badly you want to hit "send" and get it over with. Instead, at the first moment you are ready to hit "send," don't do it. Wait a few days, then proof again. We guarantee that you'll find mistakes that you missed the first time.

Don't Fret about Where Others Apply

Applicants become very protective about "their schools." If they find out that Ginny Genius is also applying to their top choice, they're heartbroken. But colleges have huge applicant pools and don't operate on a quota system that says that only one student from a particular high school can get in. If your interests are different from Ginny's, you may be competing in a totally different segment of the applicant pool.

Don't Apply Just to See If You'll Get In

Talk about a waste of time and effort. And not just yours; the high school counselor and the admissions office will also need to pull extra duty. Doesn't everyone already have enough work to do? If you know you wouldn't go if admitted, don't apply.

Don't Try to Pull Strings

It's nice that your dad is on a first-name basis with your local Congressman, but that fact will not help you get in. If your grandparents gave the school $10 million, that will help.

Don't Get Post-ED Procrastination

When students apply early decision (or early action), they should understand that the process doesn't end with filing the first application. Smart applicants keep working on their other applications until they get an ED acceptance.

✔ EXPLAINING A BUMP IN THE ROAD

Many applicants have a dip in their academic performance at some point in their high school careers. Often, there is a good reason. If you cratered in the spring of tenth grade because of mono, share that fact on your application. Any temporary situation that caused you to slump is worth noting. Even if you simply didn't work hard, it is always better to explain than to leave them guessing. If you can make a convincing case as to why your performance is better now, and will continue to be better in the future, you'll enhance your application.

"Loving your safeties is important and hard. Some kids don't visit safer schools or do as careful a job with those applications. Then they wind up getting waitlisted instead of admitted."

—SCHOOL COUNSELOR

"Don't be intimidated by people who claim that they can get in anywhere they want."

CORNELL UNIVERSITY STUDENT

"Parents can help you look back on what you have accomplished and find your unique characteristics."

BOSTON COLLEGE STUDENT

"Give yourself enough time to do the Common App supplements because they take much longer than you expect."

OHIO WESLEYAN UNIVERSITY STUDENT

✔ TEENS AND DEADLINES

Perhaps we should begin by defining the phrase "plenty of time." To an adult, plenty of time to complete a major task might be six months, three months, or in a pinch, one month. To a teen, plenty of time could be a day, or even a few hours. Therein lies the confusion when teens assure parents that they have "plenty of time" to complete their applications. To avoid driving each other crazy, parents and teens must arrive at an understanding about their differing perceptions of time. Teens must understand that there are real benefits to completing tasks before the last minute, even when there seems to be plenty of time. Parents must realize that they see things from an adult perspective, and that teens will, in fact, get most things done on their own timetable. Try to listen to each other and avoid unnecessary acrimony or panic.

✔ THE COLLEGE SEARCH, GRADE 12

Tempers can flare as deadlines approach. Help your son or daughter keep everything in perspective.

Limit Your College Talk

Nothing is more suffocating for a teen than nightly rehashing of where the college search stands. A conversation once a week should suffice. Don't blurt every time that you think of a new issue; save the college talk for a relatively relaxed time when you can address all the issues at once. As deadlines approach, your sense of urgency should increase.

Be Careful Sharing Your Preferences

You never know how your teen will react. Dutiful first children might try to follow your wishes instead of their own. Rebellious second ones may try to do the opposite of what you want. Neither dynamic is helpful. Let your son's or daughter's preferences evolve on their own.

Stay in Contact with the School Counselor

If you feel like nagging someone, call the school counselor. If your child attends a private school, it is the counselor's job to be a buffer between you and the applicant. Public-school counselors help as time permits. Counselors have seen it all before and can give you much-needed perspective.

Help Narrow Down the List

Students often have trouble getting from ten or twelve options to six or seven. Making crucial decisions before filing applications can make the final choice more manageable. No applicant ever ends up saying, "If only I had filed that tenth application…."

Give Nudges about College Essays

Essays are the lion's share of the work that goes into college applications. After these come together, everything else is easy. A month before the deadline, the student should have started the essay. If he or she seems blocked, suggest a meeting with the counselor to brainstorm.

Monitor Application Due Dates

It is the teen's responsibility to monitor the deadlines, but you should know them, too. Teens can lose track of them and can be less than forthcoming when the pressure is on. Via the Web, applications can be sent until midnight of the due date. In other words, "plenty of time."

Track ED and EA Financial Aid Process

If your son or daughter is applying early and needs financial aid, you may be required to file the CSS/PROFILE form from the College Board. Check the college's instructions for early applicants or visit www.collegeboard.org for information.

Proofread College Essays

Most applicants are comfortable with their parents reading their essays, and if yours is, you should take the opportunity. Make plenty of comments and flag errors, but avoid writing anything yourself. If your child doesn't want you to read the essay, don't take it personally. The smartest applicants are sometimes reticent about showing their work, particularly to a parent. In this case, ask that they do show it to at least one adult such as a teacher or counselor.

Track Mail and Email

Important information still occasionally comes via snail mail, but most of it is now online. You may need to prompt your son or daughter to check the email periodically. Teens are so oriented toward instant communication that email sometimes gets forgotten.

Crack the Whip

There may come a time when you must lay down the law—for instance, if your son or daughter is still procrastinating a week or two before the deadline. Do so reluctantly, but if all else fails, there may be no choice. Keep your eyes open for signs of a stress meltdown. Sometimes the issues are more serious than garden-variety procrastination.

> "Some parents call the admissions office constantly. Others talk too much during the tours. Worse yet, some try to construct emails, as the student, from the student email account. Yikes!!!"
> —School Counselor

> "We had a goal to be done by November 15 and do early action for all schools that had it. Our daughter worked hard during the summer so we could get this accomplished. I bugged her frequently. I can be annoying."
> —UNIVERSITY OF TEXAS AT AUSTIN MOM

> "If you're applying anywhere that requires a portfolio review, begin putting material together as soon as you read this. There is no such thing as too soon."

SUNY/PURCHASE STUDENT

Students

✔ GET TO KNOW THE ADMISSIONS OFFICERS

College applicants tend to think of themselves as the sum of their test scores and grades. They write essays and ask for recommendations, but in their heart of hearts, they think of themselves as a 3.88 or a 2200 (combined) when comparing themselves to other applicants. Newsflash: There are real people on the other side of the college application curtain, trying their darnedest to understand the people behind the scores.

☐ Reach out by email if you have a question.

☐ Send a personal note with your application.

- Meet the admissions officers in person as many times as possible, and follow up.

- Keep in mind that if an admissions officer remembers your sincere interest, he or she is more likely to be on your side when the admissions committee is reading applications.

✔ GET INFORMED ABOUT THE PERFORMING ARTS APPLICATION PROCESS

Like athletes, performing artists often need an extra hand from their parents in managing the application process. Dealing with the drama, dance, or music program—often in addition to the main admissions office—adds extra hoops to jump through. Here is what you need to know:

- Arts programs are not noted for their efficiency in processing applications, and they tend to be less flexible when things go astray. Keep this in mind when helping your son or daughter prepare the application materials.

- Understand that if your son or daughter wants to be a performer, he or she will most likely be required to audition, in person, either on the campus or at a regional audition conducted by traveling staff.

Since the window for auditions is typically in late January or February, look ahead for potential scheduling conflicts with other college search and application duties. Hard choices must sometimes be made.

Remember that the logistics of audition trips adds to the stress of the application process, as does choosing and rehearsing the material that the student will present. Know what to expect and be prepared.

In early fall, get out the calendar, surf the websites, and begin planning for a mid-winter crunch.

"I wish I had started earlier looking for outside, independent scholarships."

UNIVERSITY OF PENNSYLVANIA STUDENT

> "Pay attention to whether deadlines are 'send by' or 'received by.'"

UNIVERSITY OF NOTRE DAME STUDENT

✔ THE SCHOLARSHIP SEARCH

Students

With all the fuss about getting in, the scholarship search can get lost in the shuffle. Don't miss out on these great opportunities just because you're busy. You'll regret it when you're paying back your student loans.

■ **Target Colleges That Offer Merit Awards**
Ninety-five percent of money for college comes from the institution where you enroll. To increase your chances of getting a merit scholarship, consider moderately selective colleges where you are likely to be near the top of the applicant pool. Small liberal arts colleges in the Midwest are an excellent bet.

■ **Where Did Last Year's Students Get Scholarships?**
Find out from your guidance counselor about scholarships earned by students in last year's class. Many schools

track this information and can tell you the GPAs and test scores of students who got awards of particular amounts at particular colleges.

Look Local for Outside Scholarships
After the colleges, your second source for scholarship money should be local foundations and civic groups. National scholarships are much harder to get than state or local ones, a few of which may even go begging for applicants. Again, visit the guidance office for information.

Check Mom and Dad's Affiliations
Occasionally, corporations will offer awards for the children of their employees. If your parents belong to civic organizations, check those as well. Your church is also a possibility. Lutherans, in particular, sponsor a number of awards.

Reuse Your Essays
Looking for outside scholarships may seem like a lot of work, but once you have applied for one or two, it gets easier. You can often use the same essays and activity lists. Since scholarship deadlines are often later than those for admission, you can use the essays you wrote for the colleges, too.

THE WEB'S LARGEST SCHOLARSHIP SEARCH

At www.fastweb.com, you'll find leads to hundreds of thousands of scholarship awards. Most are either extremely competitive or have very specialized requirements, but it's worth a shot. After you enter information about yourself, the site will send you emails about relevant scholarships.

✔ SURVIVING THE ESSAY

Standardized tests are the biggest boogeyman of the college search, but at least they are over in three hours. Essay agony can stretch for months. For a comprehensive look at the essay-writing process, check out *Fiske Real College Essays That Work*. Key pointers include the following.

Be Likable, Not Impressive

Essays are the place to introduce yourself, not say how great you are or how you became the wonderful person you are today. (Your activities and recommendations will take care of that.) The best essays are generally humble and down-to-earth.

Write about Something Small

Don't try to think of an experience that changed your life. Instead, tell a story that sheds light on how you live day to day. The best essays generally don't labor through abstract lessons learned. They tell about real life in concrete detail. If the goal is to introduce yourself, there doesn't need to be a lesson learned.

Think Metaphorically

Personal essays always risk sounding self-important—and nine times out of ten, teenage life does not reveal universal truths. Metaphors are a good way to tell a story without being grandiose. A simple example: one successful applicant we know compared his elementary years to ancient Rome, his middle school years to the middle ages, and his high school career to the Renaissance.

Wrestle with Uncertainty

The most appealing essays come from applicants who admit that they haven't figured everything out. Nobody has. "Real" means conveying your humanity, which often depends on being honest about fears and insecurities. Colleges like students who are still growing.

Open with Flair

The first paragraph is by far the most important one. Polish it like a gemstone. People who have read lots of essays—admissions officers—can't help making a judgment about you in the first few lines. Think hard about the first impression these lines will make.

Be Sure It Has a Focus

Some essays meander from one topic to another; others begin with one focus and morph midway through into an essay about something else. Once you have an essay on paper, trim out the parts that don't fit with your main idea. Cutting is hard but necessary.

Don't Resist Starting Over

Sometimes, an essay topic just doesn't work. Unfortunately, this fact may not become clear until you have already written the essay. Rather than trying to save an essay that is doomed, the smart move is to chuck it and start over. The time you spent hasn't been wasted; you've learned some lessons for the next draft.

Focus on the "Why Us?" Essay

Many applications require students to explain why they are interested in a particular school. Applicants tend to put off this one until the last minute. That's a bad idea: Many colleges use how well students know them to measure their strength as applicants.

Set It Aside

When you have been staring at your essay for a long time, errors have a way of blending into the good stuff. If you put away the essay for a week and look at it again, you may see things that were invisible when you wrote it, from misspellings to completely unnecessary or poorly written pages.

Don't Trust Spell-Check

Applicants who run spell-check and think they have proofed their essays are in for a rude awakening.

Spell-check catches words that are misspelled, but it doesn't flag instances when words have been left out or used incorrectly.

"If your favorite activity is outside your intended major, don't be afraid to write about it."

WILLIAMS COLLEGE STUDENT

"Had I given myself more time, I think I could have written a more interesting essay."

RHODES COLLEGE STUDENT

"Pay attention to the word or character limits. Nothing is worse than having to cut chunks of your essay."

UNIVERSITY OF NOTRE DAME STUDENT

Students

✔ IS IT OK TO USE "I"?

Remember that college essays are personal essays—with an emphasis on *personal*. Your tenth grade history teacher may have told you never to use "I," but in a personal essay, you always use it.

"It wasn't until I wrote a ton of essays that I found out what I wanted to say and how to say it."

DARTMOUTH COLLEGE STUDENT

✔ COLLEGE ESSAY DON'T LIST

Even the smartest students are capable of writing nightmarish essays. Avoid this fate.

Don't Make Everything Peachy Keen

Many students edit out of their essays any sign of uncertainty or discord. But there are no perfect people, and if there were, they would write boring essays. Better to take an honest look at the good and the bad.

Don't Pretend You Were Hit by Lightning

Essay questions that talk about "significant experiences" make students believe that they must write about a life-changing event. Most people don't have experiences like this, but that doesn't stop hapless applicants from straining to write about them.

Don't Sound Flip or Nonchalant

Humor is okay, if it's funny, but sarcasm is generally not good. Seventeen-year-old cynics are not the most appealing people. The best way to be funny is to poke humor at yourself; mockery aimed at others can fall flat.

Don't Point Fingers

If you are talking about a dip in your academic performance, never place even the slightest blame on the school or teachers. If you're talking about a disciplinary incident, take full responsibility. If you must discuss circumstances that put others in a negative light, talk to your counselor and consider having him or her put it in a letter of recommendation.

Don't Let Your Parents Write It

In the days of paper applicants, the kiss of death was when two kinds of handwriting appeared on the application. Today, the fingerprints of Mom or Dad are less obvious, but they still show up in essays that lose the applicant's voice, or suddenly morph into the voice of a fifty-year-old.

> "Parents should avoid helping too much with the essays. Some essays sound like they were written by a fifty-two-year-old attorney."
> —SCHOOL COUNSELOR

> "Keep track of essays you may be able to reuse or alter for another school."

COLLEGE OF WILLIAM AND MARY STUDENT

"Make sure you click the 'submit' button. One of my friends had a misfortune because of not doing that."

TRINITY UNIVERSITY STUDENT

✔ THE FINANCIAL AID PROCESS

Though students can help, parents should take the lead in applying for aid:

Gather Tax Documents Early

Ideally, you will be able to apply for financial aid based on completed tax forms for the calendar year that ends immediately before aid applications are due. Anything you can do to speed along your W-2s and 1099s will help. Gather other relevant documents such as information on untaxed income, bank accounts, debts, and investments.

Check Financial Aid Deadlines

The spectrum is from about January 15 to March 1; the deadline at selective private colleges is often February 1. Filing a few days past the deadline probably won't make a difference, but if you will be more than a week late, you should probably file using an income estimate.

Get a FAFSA Worksheet

The Free Application for Federal Student Aid (FAFSA) is the government's aid form, required by all colleges. Filing occurs online, but every November, the government ships paper FAFSA worksheets to guidance offices. These can also be printed from www.fafsa.ed.gov. The worksheet can be helpful in guiding you through the process and make it easy for you to transfer data to the online form.

Go to www.fafsa.ed.gov and Get PINs

Check out the website of the FAFSA at least a few weeks before the aid deadline. Your first order of business should be to secure signature PIN numbers for both you and your student. These can take a few days to get and are necessary for the filing process.

See If You Need the CSS/PROFILE

A few dozen of the nation's most selective institutions require a second aid form, the PROFILE, issued by the College Board. It goes into detail about home equity, retirement accounts, noncustodial parents, and other information not included in the FAFSA. Go to www.collegeboard.org.

Consider Filing Based on Income Estimates

If you're self-employed or can't get your taxes done until spring, you'll have no choice but to do so. All will be well if you can estimate your income within a few hundred dollars, but if you're significantly off, your eligibility will need to be recalculated, which could delay your financial aid awards.

Double-Check Social Security Numbers

The worst mistake you can make on an aid application is to enter the wrong Social Security number for your student or yourself. You'll need a do-over on the whole process, and it will take time to get everything straight.

Choose Colleges to Receive a Report

Initially, you can choose up to six schools to receive a report from your aid filing. Once you get your student aid report (SAR) by return email, you can forward the results to any additional colleges that you could not designate when you filed initially.

Hit Send and Get Your EFC

After you have filled in every line of the FAFSA and hit "send," you will quickly receive your SAR, and most importantly, your expected family contribution (EFC). If the total cost of a year at college exceeds the EFC, you qualify for aid. Whether you actually get aid, and how much, will depend on the colleges.

Inform Colleges of Special Circumstances

If you need to communicate anything outside the form—for instance, a medical condition that may be expensive in the future—you should write the aid offices directly. Fax a one-page letter to each, outlining your circumstances. Aid administrators can adjust the aid formula if they have good reason.

> "I have had families with an aid package from one school have it matched by another."
> —SCHOOL COUNSELOR

> "After comparing our financial/scholarship situation with other parents and students, we now realize that we should have filed the FAFSA and CSS profile."
> —WASHINGTON UNIVERSITY IN ST. LOUIS MOM

✔ ARE ADMISSIONS NEED-BLIND?

Students

It used to be one of the catchphrases of the college search: need-blind admissions. It meant that no matter what your family finances, you would receive the same consideration for admission as any other applicant. But most colleges have quietly moved away from that policy, and today, no more than a handful of the nation's most selective colleges are actually need-blind. How does this trend impact you? If you are a borderline applicant and have high need, the odds are greater that you will not be admitted than they would be if your family could pay the whole bill. Still apply to those elite colleges, but also include some less selective ones in your mix, where you might be above average and therefore have a better shot at admission. Of course, you could simply decide not to apply for aid at Highly Selective U., but if you did get in, do you really want to graduate with a mountain of debt? It is better to be honest about your family's financial need and find a college that will meet it.

✔ IS AID A REALISTIC HOPE?

Families earning roughly $75,000 to $200,000 in annual income have often been disappointed with the financial aid process. But a promising change is afoot at some of the nation's richest colleges. Led by Harvard, most of them have increased the amount of aid awarded to families in this income range. Just as importantly, these policies have legitimized the idea that a family earning up to $200,000 per year can, in some circumstances, qualify for significant aid. A struggling economy may put a dent in some of these efforts. But even if you think applying for aid will be a waste of time, do it anyway. You never know.

> "The big moves by schools such as Stanford and Columbia (and many more) to enhance need-based aid for middle-income families have been terrifically well-received."
>
> —SCHOOL COUNSELOR

ONE-STOP SOURCE FOR AID INFORMATION

The Web's best site for aid information is the Smart Student Guide to Financial Aid at www.finaid.org. It includes information about every aspect of the aid process, as well as an eligibility estimator and information on loans and 529 saving plans.

Students

✔ WINTER OF SENIOR YEAR

You're a second-semester senior, and life is good. Just keep in mind a few to-dos:

■ **Revisit Local Scholarships**

When you're through applying to colleges and have caught up on schoolwork, take another look at scholarship opportunities in your community. If you're not a straight-A student, look for essay contests.

Monitor Your Application Status

You can get updates on your applications at the college websites, or if that fails, by calling to see if your application is complete. Do not panic if a piece of the application is missing. It can take weeks for colleges to assemble all the application materials, including online applications, mailed transcripts and test scores, letters of recommendation, etc. If something gets lost, it can be resent.

Keep a Strong Academic Schedule

When the second semester begins, resist the temptation to drop challenging classes. Most of the pressure is off, but that doesn't mean you can go into the tank. A big change in your schedule may require an explanation to the college that accepts you. And if you're waitlisted, you may need to send third-quarter grades.

Don't Get Cs, Ds, or Fs

If you get two or more of the latter, you can probably kiss your admission good-bye. Colleges reserve the right to rescind offers to students who fall apart during the second semester. If you get Cs and Ds, expect a stern letter and perhaps probation as you begin your college career.

Keep Thinking about Colleges

If you have a first-choice college at the moment, there is still time to change your mind several more times. If there is any college on your application list that you do not know well, learn more about it. Consider making a few college visits. Keep your head in the game and you'll be able to make a more informed choice in April.

"Always follow up with the colleges to make sure they have all your materials. Multiple schools didn't receive mine."

COLUMBIA COLLEGE (IL) STUDENT

"Make sure your son or daughter applies to several 'safety schools,' preferably ones that will let you know by December. Having your child accepted to at least one school reduces stress tremendously."

—UNIVERSITY OF VIRGINIA DAD

> "I got into my reaches and regret not reaching higher."

WAGNER COLLEGE STUDENT

Students

✔ AFTER THE ACCEPTANCES

Celebrate for a day or two, but then get back to reality. There's still a lot of work ahead.

☐ **Visit Where You Got In**

Most colleges roll out the red carpet for accepted applicants. We recommend that you go to as many of these events as possible. A campus looks different after you get in, and you'll have a good chance to connect with faculty. More importantly, you'll get to meet your future classmates.

☐ **Evaluate Aid Awards**

Do this with the help of your parents. No one would recommend that you make your final choice based on a few hundred dollars here or there, but if another college's aid award beats the one from your first choice, it will make sense to appeal for more aid. If such aid is not forthcoming, would you be willing to help your parents pay the difference in order to attend your top choice?

Go Online

The Web is full of accepted students who want to talk to others who have gotten in at the same places. Colleges' websites usually have password-protected areas where students can go. Or, log in to your favorite social networking site and connect with your potential classmates.

Make a Chart or Go with Your Gut

There is no right way to make your decision about which college to attend. Some applicants take a highly organized approach; others simply choose the one that feels right. Try not to be too influenced by your friends. Once you arrive on campus, you'll probably go your separate ways.

Don't Mess with May 1

When colleges send out offers of admission, they make a guess about how many students will accept. If more students want to enroll than they expect, colleges risk running out of dorm space. In a year when too many applicants are saying "yes," colleges sometimes close the door on students who do not reply by May 1.

"Go with your instincts and not your parents' instincts."

LAFAYETTE COLLEGE STUDENT

"Pick the school you liked best on your overnight visit."

KUTZTOWN UNIVERSITY STUDENT

Parents

✔ APPEALING FOR MORE AID

If you believe the colleges have overlooked important circumstances, or if your financial situation is changing, fax a one-page letter of appeal to the aid offices and then follow up with a phone call. Your best ammunition will be if your son or daughter got a better offer from a similar institution. (Fax a copy of the other school's award.) Williams College will not be impressed if you get a merit scholarship from Framingham State, but it would probably match an offer from Amherst College.

✔ DO YOUR "DEAR JOHN" EMAILS

Students

It is natural to focus on where you want to go at this exciting time, but make sure you're prompt in informing the other colleges that you are not coming. Do it as soon as you have eliminated them from consideration. Students on waitlists around the nation will be grateful, since their acceptance may come only after you have bowed out.

✔ HANDLING THE WAITLIST

Students

More and more students are finding themselves on waitlists. Let the offers settle in for a few days. But by April 15, if you're planning to pursue the waitlist, you should be moving full speed.

Do You Really Want It?

The regular admission process has enough agony for most students. The waitlist can prolong it through May, and sometimes into the summer. The odds are usually less than 50-50 on a waitlist, but circumstances vary. Many students decide that they will be happier at a college that accepted them in the first round, which is a good way to avoid waitlist stress.

Talk to Your Counselor

Your counselor can be a vital advocate. He or she can call the college to sound out your chances and help you plot strategy. If the counselor has advice on whether or not you should pursue the waitlist at a particular college, take it seriously.

Go After Your Top Choice

Don't try to stay on three or four waitlists. Colleges want to know that waitlisted students will enroll if admitted. You can't honestly make that claim at more than one or two. To have a good chance on the waitlist, you need to be aggressive. Forthright interest can help you get in.

Write an (Email) Letter

Send it to the admissions officer in charge of your region of the country, and make the case that the school is a good match. Consider making a visit where you could meet with an admissions officer, especially if you have not had a campus interview.

Send Updates

Your third-quarter grades should be sent, along with an update on your activities if there is anything new. Occasionally, an additional recommendation can help if you have a twelfth-grade teacher who knows you well.

> "Colleges are putting more pressure on students to deposit early, and they're using their waitlists more."
> —SCHOOL COUNSELOR

> "The amazing beauty of the American college system is the wide variety of programs available to fit every need."
> —DUKE UNIVERSITY MOM

✔ AFTER THE ACCEPTANCES

There may be celebration; there may be tears. For parents, the key is not to get too high or too low.

Mute Your Reactions

Let your student sort out his or her reaction to the decisions without your influence. You may have personal favorites, and there will be a time to express your preferences. First, listen to what your son or daughter has to say.

Be a Sounding Board

Your goal should not be to tell your child what to do, but rather to help him or her make a decision. Try to facilitate critical thinking about the choice. If you believe that he or she is putting too much emphasis on a particular factor in the decision, say so.

Support Last-Minute Visits
These have become an increasingly important part of the selection process in recent years. College-sponsored visit days often have programming for parents as well as students. If you do go, let your child have plenty of space to enjoy the campus and mingle with future classmates.

Help Scrutinize Aid Awards
It isn't just the total amount of the package that matters. How much loan is included? Are the loans subsidized? Is there an allowance in the budget for living expenses and travel to and from the college? If possible, sit down with the guidance counselor to go over these details.

Send the Deposit
Students must send in a deposit to a college that has accepted them by May 1, even if they are on a waitlist elsewhere. The deposit is usually nonrefundable. It is understood that students on a waitlist at another college may eventually withdraw if the college that waitlisted them offers admission. The deposit is the cost of doing so.

"We felt that this had to be our daughter's decision and that she would handle any negative issues at the college better knowing that she made the decision to go there."

—SANTA CLARA UNIVERSITY MOM

"A well-motivated student can get a good education from any school."

—UNIVERSITY OF PUGET SOUND DAD

DECIPHERING FINANCIAL AID PACKAGES

Created by a reporter from *U.S. News & World Report*, www. FinancialAidLetter.com features real award letters with notes written by experts. The site is an excellent guide to financial aid jargon and the ways that aid letters can mislead unsuspecting readers.

✔ THE PERILS OF PLUS LOANS

One word in an aid package should set off alarm bells: PLUS. Colleges often pad their aid packages with PLUS loans, which are parent loans that anyone can get regardless of need and which are offered at market rates. In other words, PLUS loans aren't really financial aid. Yet some families are encouraged to borrow $10,000 per year or more using PLUS. We recommend against it; student loans, which your student will pay back, should be the bulk of your borrowing. If you do consider a PLUS loan, compare it to other options such as borrowing against your home.

Students

✔ HOW MUCH DEBT IS TOO MUCH?

It may be necessary to take out loans in order to go to Dream U. Hopefully, your freshman-year package will include not more than $5,000 in loans. Since the loan amount will probably go up in future years, you'll be looking at a substantial, but manageable, debt of not more than $20,000 to $25,000 for four years of study. Any loan amount above $5,000 for the first year, whether it's loans for students or parents, is problematic.

"Find time in this last summer before college to sit and laugh as a family. Laugh about the ball of nerves everyone has; laugh about how Mom (or Dad) continues to run the show. Allow for these lovely, naturally sad but essential moments to be without pressure."

—SCHOOL COUNSELOR

✔ THE SUMMER BEFORE COLLEGE

This should be one of the best times of your life. Have fun with your friends and enjoy a relatively stress-free summer before college starts. Many colleges, especially public universities, have orientation in the summer, allowing you to see the place with your parents before you come back for real. Smaller private colleges usually have orientation in the fall, though often with a variety of possibilities for group bonding experiences. We recommend that you carefully consider these opportunities.

Your most important practical task is to pack. Below is a list of the top ten things you will need but are likely to forget:

Bathrobe

You'll probably need to walk through common space between the shower and your room.

Reading Light

Unless your roommate goes to bed when you do—highly unlikely—a small light to affix near your bed will come in handy.

Milk Crates

Put books in them, haul stuff in them, stack them, stand on them to replace a light bulb. Few items are more versatile.

Power Strip

Old dorms often don't have enough electrical outlets for today's students.

Duct Tape

Use it anywhere and everywhere.

Quarters

Some colleges have high-tech dryers that use swipe cards. Others still have the kind that takes quarters.

Mini Tool Kit

From hanging pictures to hooking up electronic gadgets, dorm life requires a few simple tools.

Dry Erase Board

It is nice to have a place on your door to leave messages when you are gone.

Raincoat

People in college need to walk in all kinds of weather. You need a good raincoat.

Thick Socks

We mean the kind with tread on the bottom. There will probably be a lot of padding around without shoes on.

"Read all the fine print in all the literature that is sent with the acceptance letter. That's where I learned that most freshmen are assigned to a triple room, but the stated price for room and board was for a double room, which makes our cost actually less."
—UNIVERSITY OF PUGET SOUND MOM

IF YOU'RE WORRIED ABOUT FORGETTING SOMETHING...

Log on to www.keepandshare.com, where you'll find a college packing list that spans two hundred items and ideas for outfitting your dorm room.

✔ LETTING GO

For some parents, the admissions process is the easy part. The summer after twelfth grade is an emotional time, but also a happy one.

Pay the Bill

Be sure to take care of your first payment well before the start of the school year. The bureaucratic wheels can grind slowly, and if the bursar's office is not showing that it has received your check, your son or daughter may not be able to register for classes.

Expect Conflict

Don't fret if you are at loggerheads with your child. As the time of leaving approaches, many families have an upsurge in emotion due to the feeling of impending loss. Try to stay as level-headed as possible under the likely onslaught of emotion.

Talk about Credit Cards and Spending

From the day they set foot on campus, college students are bombarded by people hawking credit cards. Set some ground rules in the summer; if the student is going to get a card, what kind? Make sure he knows the basics, like the fact that if he pays off the balance in full, he doesn't have to pay the (outrageous) interest fees.

Follow Up on Housing and Course Registration

Help your son or daughter make sure that none of the logistical details fall through the cracks. If your daughter wants a quiet dorm, it would be bad for her to spend freshman year in Animal House because she lost track of a housing deadline. Some of this may be accomplished at summer orientation.

Encourage Optional Orientation Programs

Everyone gets an orientation, but sometimes there are additional programs you can sign up for. Many colleges sponsor backpacking trips, for instance, that include a segment of the freshman class and help students make friends before moving to campus. Such programs are almost always worthwhile.

Go to Parent Orientation Programs

Nowadays, colleges understand that parents are their customers, too. Most have orientations for you as well as your son or daughter. You can learn about contact people at the college and network with other parents.

Help Size Up Dorm Needs

One benefit of summer orientation is the chance to see your student's dorm room, or at least a generic one, before the move-in date. If orientation is in the fall, immediately before classes begin, you may want to take a peek inside and then run to a store if you see potential needs.

Use Electronic Communication

Phoning a college student can be dicey. Aside from their crazy hours, you never know when you will catch them in a room full of friends, or at some other time where "Hi Mom" is the last thing they want coming out of their mouths. Email is always a safe option.

Expect Teary Phone Calls

Every student calls home in distress at some point. Listen, stay calm, and try not to worry about it. The problems will likely be forgotten by the next call. Never entertain the idea of letting the student come home, or of transferring, until at least the winter break.

Know Whom You Can Contact

Occasionally, college freshmen do have serious problems. If those problems persist for weeks or months, you should contact someone in student affairs. Often, they can ask a (student) resident advisor to check things out. Colleges are more responsive to parental concerns than in previous generations.

"No matter what the average SAT scores are for their institution, most kids have the same fears—Will I fit in? Will I make friends? How will I adjust to a roommate? Sharing bathrooms? There seems to be little worry about academics and time management."

—SCHOOL COUNSELOR

"Some kids cling to parents when they arrive on campus—others want them out of there...fast!!"

—SCHOOL COUNSELOR

✔ EVERYBODY LOVES A CARE PACKAGE

The best thing any parent can do—dads, too—is to send a care package. Homemade treats and any other edible fare are always crowd-pleasers. If you pack enough to share, you're guaranteed to help your student make a few new friends.

✔ PARENTAL CONTACT ON YOUR TERMS

Your parents, rightly, have the expectation that you will keep in touch on a regular basis. If you don't, they'll try to reach you, which can lead to frustration if they catch you at awkward times or can't connect and get worried. Once you know your schedule, suggest a time for a phone call once a week, or at some other interval that makes sense.

"After May 1, the clamor of college admissions suddenly goes off the radar screen. The sense of something being lost (innocence, childhood, protected environments at school and at home) becomes clear. There is little mention of the anxieties of starting college in the fall but they do exist."

—SCHOOL COUNSELOR

✔ WHEN GRADES DON'T COME IN THE MAIL

College is different from high school because grades don't come home. Some parents are surprised to learn that even though they are paying the bills, they don't have the legal right to request grades from the colleges. If your son or daughter seems overly secretive about grades, try to find out why. If you suspect trouble, you can make discreet inquiries through the office of student affairs.

✔ BE PATIENT DURING FRESHMAN YEAR

After years of hearing that college will be the best time of your life, the reality of homesickness and loneliness that can hit during the freshman year is often a letdown. Give it time. In truth, freshman year may be one of the most difficult of your life, but it gets better with time. Also, have patience with your new friendships. It will take time for you to develop the sort of bonds that you have with high school friends.

epilogue

✔ BACK TO WHAT REALLY MATTERS

Does getting into Harvard make people happy? With all the hype surrounding the college search, it would be logical to assume that admission to the world's most prestigious university would ensure a lifetime of satisfaction and pride.

But it doesn't. Students at Harvard—or any other elite university—are no more or less happy than the students anywhere else. Some students there find meaning and fulfillment; others lead lives of stressed-out desperation. The majority have their ups and downs but are reasonably content, just like students everywhere.

Take advantage of the pause between high school and college to think about what really matters. What kind of person do you want to be? If you were a ball of stress in high school, how is college going to be different? For one of the few times in your life, you will have the chance to reinvent yourself.

Now is also a good time to take stock of where you've been—your friends, family, and your home. In the summer before college, be sure to spend plenty of time with everyone who is important in your life. Once you leave for college, things will change, and the world you know now will be gone.

Happiness and success in college have much less to do with where you go to college than with what you make of it once there. The admission process, with its highs and lows, was just an opening act. The main event is yet to come.

college counselors advisory group

Marilyn Albarelli, Moravian Academy (PA)

Scott Anderson, St. George's Independent School (TN)

Christine Asmussen, St. Andrew's-Sewanee School (TN)

Bruce Bailey, Lakeside School (WA)

Amy E. Belstra, Cherry Creek H.S. (CO)

Greg Birk, Kinkaid School (TX)

Susan T. Bisson, Advocates for Human Potential (MA)

Francine E. Block, American College Admissions Consultants (PA)

Robin Boren, Education Consultant (CO)

Clarice Boring, Cody H.S. (WY)

John B. Boshoven, Community High School & Jewish Academy of Metro Detroit (MI)

Mimi Bradley, St. Andrew's Episcopal School (MS)

Claire Cafaro, Clear Directions (NJ)

Nancy Caine, St. Augustine H.S. (CA)

Jane M. Catanzaro, College Advising Services (CT)

Mary Chapman, St. Catherine's School (VA)

Anthony L. Clay, Durham Academy (NC)

Kathy Cleaver, Durham Academy (NC)

Jimmie Lee Cogburn, Independent Counselor (GA)

Alison Cotten, Cypress Falls H.S. (TX)

Alice Cotti, Polytechnic School (CA)

Rod Cox, St. Johns Country Day School (FL)

Kim Crockard, Crockard College Counseling (AL)

Carroll K. Davis, North Central H.S. (IN)

Mary Jo Dawson, Academy of the Sacred Heart (MI)

Lexi Eagles, Greensboro Country Day School (NC)

Dan Feldhaus, Iolani School (HI)

Ralph S. Figueroa, Albuquerque Academy (NM)

Emily E. FitzHugh, The Gunnery (CT)

Mary Fitzsimmons, Fiske Guide Workshops (NJ)

Larry Fletcher, Salesianum School (DE)

Nancy Fomby, Episcopal School of Dallas (TX)

Daniel Franklin, Education Consultant (CO)

Laura Johnson Frey, Vermont Academy (VT)

Phyllis Gill, Providence Day School (NC)

H. Scotte Gordon, Moses Brown School (RI)

Freida Gottsegen, Education Consultant (GA)

Molly Gotwals, Suffield Academy (CT)

Kathleen Barnes Grant, The Catlin Gabel School (OR)

Madelyn Gray, John Burroughs
School (MO)

Amy Grieger, Northfield Mount
Hermon School (MA)

Mimi Grossman, St. Mary's Episcopal
School (TN)

Elizabeth Hall, Education Consulting
Services (TX)

Andrea L. Hays, Education
Consultant (GA)

Darnell Heywood, Columbus
Academy (OH)

Bruce Hunter, Rowland Hall-St.
Mark's School (UT)

Deanna L. Hunter, Shawnee Mission
East H.S. (KS)

Linda King, College Connections (NY)

Sharon Koenings, Brookfield
Academy (WI)

Joan Jacobson, Shawnee Mission
South H.S. (KS)

Diane Johnson, Lawrence Public
Schools (NY)

Gerimae Kleinman, Shaker Heights
H.S. (OH)

Laurie Leftwich, Brother Martin
High School (LA)

MaryJane London, Los Angeles
Center for Enriched Studies (CA)

Martha Lyman, Deerfield Academy
(MA)

Brad MacGowan, Newton North
H.S. (MA)

Robert S. MacLellan, Jr., Hebron
Academy (ME)

Susan Marrs, The Seven Hills School
(OH)

Karen A. Mason, Wyoming Seminary
(PA)

Lynne McConnell, Rumson-Fair
Haven Regional H.S. (NJ)

Lisa Micele, University of Illinois
Laboratory H.S. (IL)

Corky Miller-Strong, The Culver
Academies (IN)

Janet Miranda, Prestonwood
Christian Academy (TX)

Joyce Vining Morgan, White
Mountain School (NH)

Judith Nash, Highland High School
(ID)

Gunnar W. Olson, Indian Springs
School (AL)

Stuart Oremus, Wellington School
(OH)

Geri Perkal, Fiske Guide Workshops
(NJ)

Deborah Robinson, Mandarin H.S.
(FL)

Julie Rollins, Episcopal H.S. (TX)

Heidi Rose, Crystal Springs Uplands
School (CA)

William C. Rowe, Thomas Jefferson
School (MO)

Bruce Scher, Chicagoland Jewish H.S.
(IL)

David Schindel, Sandia Preparatory
School (NM)

Kathy Z. Schmidt, St. Mary's Hall
(TX)

Barbara Simmons, Notre Dame High
School (CA)

Joe Stehno, Bishop Brady H.S. (NH)

Bruce Stempien, Weston H.S. (CT)

Paul M. Stoneham, The Key School
(MD)

Ted de Villafranca, Peddie School
(NJ)

Scott White, Montclair H.S. (NJ)

Linda Zimring, Los Angeles United
School District (CA)

Completely updated every year

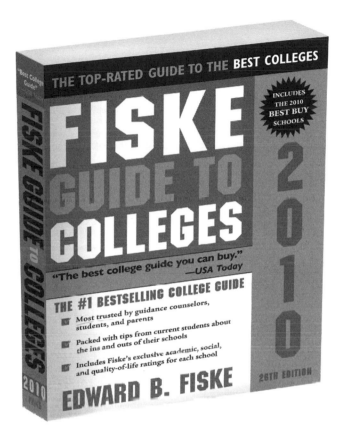

FISKE GUIDE TO COLLEGES 2010
978-1-4022-0960-4 • $22.99

The bestselling and most trusted college guide used by students, parents, and counselors across the country! The guide includes an in-depth look at more than 300 colleges and universities in the United States and abroad. It rates each school on a scale of 1 to 5 on academics, social life, and quality of life. It also describes campus culture, lists each school's best programs, and provides average SAT and ACT scores. *Fiske Guide to Colleges* is unequaled at capturing the true essence of each school while providing all the necessary statistics.

Understand the admissions process and where you fit in best

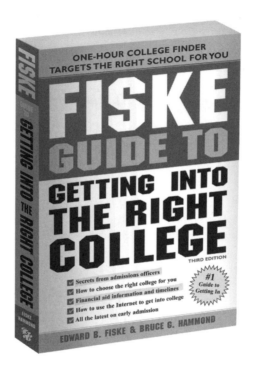

FISKE GUIDE TO GETTING INTO THE RIGHT COLLEGE
978-1-4022-0916-1 • $14.95

Fiske Guide to Getting Into the Right College takes students and parents step-by-step through the college admissions process, including selecting your top choices, interviewing, getting letters of recommendation, understanding how admission offices work, and getting the most financial aid you can. The expert advice and tips will help you get accepted at a challenging school that fits your personality and learning style.

Learn how to write the essay
that gets you accepted

FISKE REAL COLLEGE ESSAYS THAT WORK
978-1-4022-2510-9 • $14.99

From the most trusted name in college admission resources comes the first application-essay book designed for those who need it most: bright students who aren't natural writers. This all-inclusive guide to tackling the application essay provides more than 100 real sample essays, as well as tips and tools for editing from first draft to final submission.

Don't miss those deadlines!

FISKE WHAT TO DO WHEN FOR COLLEGE
978-1-4022-1047-1 • $12.95

All of the dates frazzled parents and college-bound students need are now in one place. Completely hands-on and arranged as an easy-to-follow calendar, *Fiske What to Do When for College* includes monthly overviews of what to do and all major deadlines for admissions and scholarships. Also included are narrative essays written by two of the top college experts in the country addressing what to do each week and what to think about in the coming weeks. Don't forget an important date ever again!

Matriculate with confidence

FISKE 250 WORDS EVERY HIGH SCHOOL GRADUATE NEEDS TO KNOW
978-1-4022-1841-5 • $8.99

Here are the 250 most important words students need to know to be successful in college and beyond, from the former Education Editor of the *New York Times* and a leading authority on college admissions. Each entry contains information on the word origin, a complete definition, and example sentences, making it both the perfect gift for high school graduation and an effective tool for expanding students' vocabulary, increasing word comprehension, and honing their writing skills.

Discover the words
you need to succeed

FISKE 250 WORDS EVERY HIGH SCHOOL FRESHMAN NEEDS TO KNOW
978-1-4022-1840-8 • $8.99

Starting off with a powerful vocabulary is the best way to prepare for a successful, stress-free time in high school. *Fiske 250 Words Every High School Freshman Needs to Know* will give you the tools to sharpen your writing skills and use language evocatively. Nail your English essays, the SAT and ACT writing tests, and all of your college and scholarship applications.

Learn—don't just memorize— more than 1,000 words

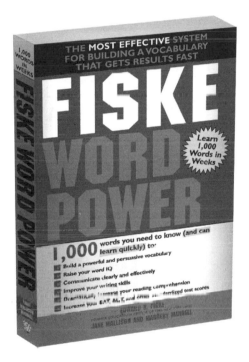

FISKE WORDPOWER
978-1-4022-0653-5 • $11.95

This amazing new system for building your vocabulary will teach students and word lovers alike to learn—not just memorize— essential words. Readers will learn thousands of new terms in weeks. *Fiske WordPower* includes more than 1,000 words and definitions, example sentences, origins and roots, plus quizzes to determine comprehension.

Find out the truth about how
to raise your SAT score

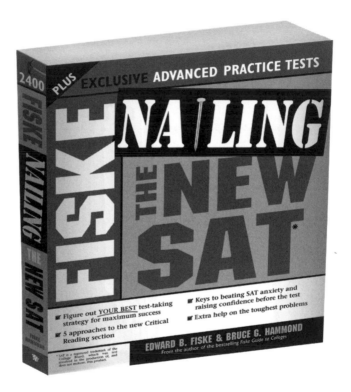

FISKE NAILING THE NEW SAT
978-1-4022-0408-1 • $16.95

What's so new about the "new SAT"? Find out with *Fiske Nailing
the New SAT*. Based on one of the largest surveys of high-scoring
SAT-takers ever conducted, the book unlocks the secrets of the
nation's most feared standardized test. The step-by-step analysis
of the hardest questions and answers prepares you for every
surprise. Includes two complete sample SATs to practice what
you've learned.